WeightWatchers®

Get set for *Summer*

Nicola Graimes

First published in Great Britain as *Simply Enjoy*
by Simon & Schuster UK Ltd, 2011

This edition first published in 2015 by
Simon & Schuster UK Ltd
A CBS Company

SIMON AND SCHUSTER
Simon & Schuster UK
222 Gray's Inn Road
London WC1X 8HB

www.simonandschuster.co.uk

Simon & Schuster Australia, Sydney
Simon & Schuster India, New Delhi

10 9 8 7 6 5 4 3 2 1

Weight Watchers, *ProPoints* and the *ProPoints* icon
are the registered trademarks of Weight Watchers
International Inc. and used under license by
Weight Watchers (UK) Ltd. All rights reserved.

Photography: Steve Baxter
Prop styling: Rachel Jukes
Food preparation: Kim Morphew
Design and typesetting: Jane Humphrey

Colour Reproduction by Aylesbury Studios Ltd, UK
Printed and bound in China

A CIP catalogue record for this book is available from
the British Library

ISBN 978-1-47114-991-7

Pictured on the front cover: Beef Kebabs in Smoky
Barbecue Sauce, page 76; Picnic Loaf, page 70
Pictured on the back cover top: Pan Catalan, page 82;
bottom from left to right: Linguine with Broad Beans
and Rocket, page 42; Cool Dogs, page 126; Vanilla and
Coconut Balls with Mango, page 148

If you would like to find out more about Weight Watchers and the
ProPoints Plan, please visit: www.weightwatchers.co.uk

Ⓥ This symbol denotes a vegetarian recipe and assumes that, where
relevant, free range eggs, vegetarian cheese, vegetarian virtually fat free
fromage frais, vegetarian low fat crème fraîche and vegetarian low fat
yogurts are used. Virtually fat free fromage frais, low fat crème fraîche and
low fat yogurts may contain traces of gelatine so they are not always
vegetarian. Please check the labels.

❄ This symbol denotes a dish that can be frozen. Unless otherwise stated,
you can freeze the finished dish for up to 3 months. Defrost thoroughly and
reheat until the dish is piping hot throughout.

Recipe notes

Egg size Medium size unless otherwise stated.

Raw eggs Only the freshest eggs should be used. Pregnant women, the
elderly and children should avoid recipes with eggs which are not fully
cooked or raw.

All fruits and vegetables Medium size unless otherwise stated.

Chocolate Use chocolate with a minimum of 70% cocoa solids.

Low fat spread Where a recipe states to use a low fat spread, a light spread
with a fat content of no less than 38% should be used.

Stock Stock cubes should be used in the recipes, unless otherwise stated.
Prepare them according to the packet instructions, unless directed
otherwise.

Microwaves Microwave timings are for an 850 watt microwave oven.

Recipe timings These are approximate and meant to be guidelines. Please
note that the preparation time includes all the steps up to and following
the main cooking time(s).

Low fat soft cheese Where a recipe states to use low fat soft cheese, a soft
cheese with a fat content of less than 5% should be used.

Nicola Graimes is an award-winning health, cookery and food writer who
has written numerous books for Weight Watchers. She lives in Brighton with
her husband and two children.

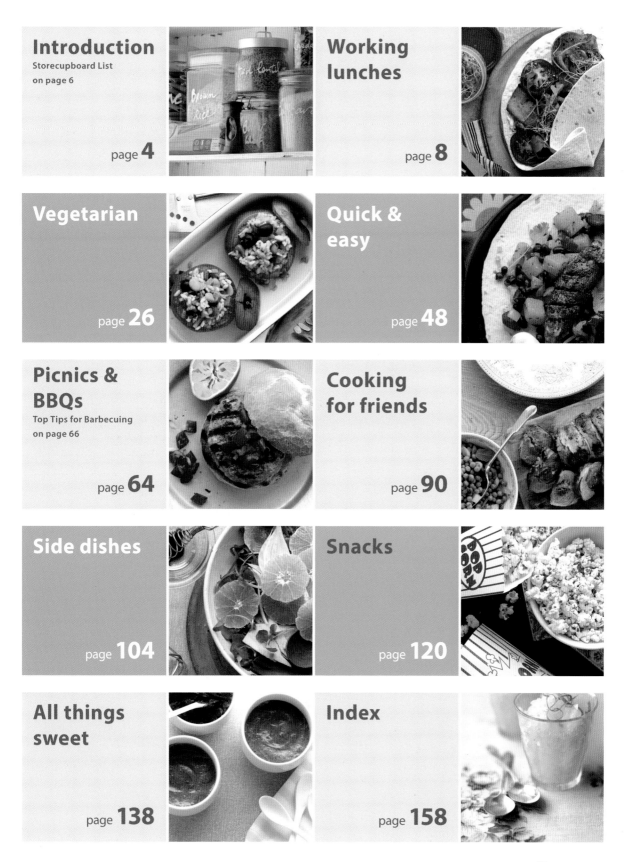

Contents 3

Ready, steady... get set for summer!

With over 100 recipes designed to work around real life – your life – *Get Set for Summer* offers you all the inspiration you need in order to be flexible and creative in planning your meals.

During the summer months, when you are spending more time outdoors with family and friends, thoughts will turn to al fresco eating: there's a whole chapter devoted to picnics and barbecues, with recipes ranging from Tear 'n' Share Tomato and Cheese Bread, Picnic Loaf and Honey Glazed Sausages to Giant 'Sausage' Roll, Beef Kebabs in Smoky Barbecue Sauce and Falafel Burgers.

And if you're looking for ideas to make the most of fresh seasonal ingredients then check out the Watermelon, Feta and Mint Salad, Sticky Duck with Nectarines, Mango and Herb Couscous, and

Barbecued Fruit with Vanilla Cream. With fabulous recipes for lunches, snacks, quick and easy meals ready in 30 minutes or under, vegetarian dishes, cooking for friends, delicious side dishes and the ever popular desserts – you'll find a glorious selection of lighter meals for the longer days, all designed to help you get the most out of your summer.

All the recipes in *Get Set for Summer* have clear step-by-step instructions, and many have helpful tips and suggestions to keep things as varied and interesting as possible. And, at the front of each chapter, there's an index listing the recipes in order of timings so, at a glance, you'll have the information you need to make planning ahead a doddle. Whether you're cooking for yourself, your family or your friends, you'll discover plenty to enjoy in this stunning cookbook.

Storecupboard list

Here's a handy list of the most common and useful ingredients to keep in your cupboard.

Baking and sweet ingredients

Baking powder

Bicarbonate of soda

Cocoa powder

Cornflour

Flour; plain, wholemeal and
self-raising

Fruit, dried

Honey

Reduced sugar jam

Sugar free jelly

Sugar; granulated, caster, icing
and brown

Vanilla extract

Whole rolled porridge oats

Basic cooking ingredients

Artificial sweetener

Black peppercorns

Calorie controlled cooking spray

Chillies, dried

Gelatine

Olive oil

Oregano, dried

Salt (preferably sea salt or low
sodium)

Sesame oil

Stock cubes; vegetable, beef
and chicken

Sunflower or vegetable oil

Basic frozen ingredients

Broad beans

French beans

Fruits

Peas

Prawns

Sweetcorn

Canned goods

Baked beans, reduced sugar
and salt

Borlotti beans

Butter beans

Canned fruit, in natural juice

Cannellini beans

Chick peas

Curry pastes

Flageolet beans

Kidney beans

Lentils

Pesto

Tomatoes, chopped

Tuna, canned in brine or
in spring water

Condiments

Apple sauce

Gravy granules

Horseradish sauce

Mayonnaise, extra light

Mint sauce

Mushrooms, dried e.g. porcini

Mustard, Dijon

Mustard, English

Mustard, wholegrain

Salad dressing, fat free

Soy sauce

Tabasco sauce

Tomato ketchup

Tomato purée

Vinegar, balsamic

Worcestershire sauce

Dried herbs and spices

Bay leaves

Cayenne pepper

Chilli powder

Chinese five spice powder

Cinnamon, ground

Coriander seeds

Cumin, ground

Cumin seeds

Curry powder

Garam masala

Ginger, ground

Mixed herbs, dried

Mixed spice, ground

Nutmeg

Paprika

Dried pasta and noodles

Egg noodles, wholemeal or white

Pasta, wholemeal or white

Rice noodles, wholemeal or white

Fresh and chilled ingredients

Cheddar cheese, reduced fat

Eggs

Fresh potted herbs for the windowsill
such as oregano, basil, mint

Soft cheese, low fat

Yogurt, 0% fat Greek

Yogurt, low fat fruit and plain

Rice and grains

Bulgur wheat

Couscous, wholemeal or plain

Rice; brown, long grain or basmati

Working lunches

Beef wrap with horseradish cream on page 10

Looking for some new ideas for quick and satisfying lunches? Why not try the Beef Wrap with Horseradish Cream or the Tuna Waldorf Pitta Pockets? They're ideal for a quick lunch at the office or at home. And with easy recipes such as Mozzarella, Tomato and Ham Quesadilla or Sesame Beef Noodles, you can enjoy great lunches anytime.

Sweet potato and chicken salad

Calories per serving 201

Takes 15 mins

Serves 2

200 g (7 oz) sweet potatoes, peeled and cut into
    1 cm (½ inch) cubes
1 celery stick, sliced finely
2.5 cm (1 inch) cucumber, quartered,
    de-seeded and sliced
100 g (3½ oz) cooked skinless chicken breast,
    cubed
¼ red onion, diced
2 sprigs of fresh mint leaves
1 Little Gem lettuce, shredded
For the dressing
2 tablespoons low fat plain yogurt
1 tablespoon extra light mayonnaise
1 tablespoon smooth mango chutney
1 teaspoon curry powder
1 tablespoon lemon juice
¼ teaspoon dried chilli flakes
salt and freshly ground black pepper

This lightly spiced salad is ideal for a quick and delicious lunch.

1 Bring a saucepan of water to the boil, add the sweet potatoes and cook for about 10 minutes or until tender. Drain, set aside and leave to cool.

2 To make the dressing, mix together all the ingredients with 1 tablespoon of water in a small bowl. Season to taste.

3 Put the sweet potatoes, celery, cucumber, chicken and red onion in a serving bowl, spoon the dressing over and toss the salad until coated. Scatter the mint over before serving on a bed of shredded lettuce.

V **Try this** Replace the chicken with 100 g (3½ oz) Quorn Chicken Style Pieces. To prepare, spray with cooking spray and stir fry for 8–10 minutes. Leave to cool before adding to the salad in step 3.

Beef wrap with horseradish cream

Calories per serving 264

Takes 5 mins

Serves 1

1 large low fat tortilla wrap (about 19 cm/
    7½ inches in diameter)
1 teaspoon horseradish sauce
1 teaspoon extra light mayonnaise
50 g (1¾ oz) thin slice cooked roast beef
1 tomato, sliced into rounds
a small handful of rocket leaves
a small handful of alfalfa sprouts
freshly ground black pepper

A novel idea for using up leftover meat from the Sunday roast.

1 Put the tortilla in a large, dry, non stick frying pan and heat gently for about 2 minutes, turning once, until warmed through (this will make the tortilla easier to fold).

2 Mix together the horseradish and mayonnaise and spread over the tortilla. Place the roast beef on one side of the tortilla then top with the tomato, rocket and alfalfa sprouts. Season, then fold in each side and roll up to encase the filling.

3 Cut the tortilla in half diagonally, leave to cool and either eat immediately or wrap tightly in cling film or baking parchment if taking to work.

Variation The same weight of skinless roast chicken or cooked lean pork can be used instead of the beef to make this wrap.

Tuna Waldorf pitta pockets

Calories per serving 290

Takes 15 mins

Serves 2

4 shelled walnut halves
90 g (3¼ oz) tuna in spring water, drained and
  flaked
½ apple, unpeeled and grated
1 small celery stick, chopped finely
25 g (1 oz) red cabbage, shredded
2 wholemeal pitta bread
2 round lettuce leaves
For the dressing
2 tablespoons fat free plain fromage frais
1 tablespoon extra light mayonnaise
1 tablespoon lemon juice
¼ teaspoon finely grated lemon zest
salt and freshly ground black pepper

All the ingredients of a classic Waldorf salad and more are wrapped up in these tasty pittas. They're great for work too.

1 Toast the walnut halves in a dry non stick frying pan for about 3 minutes, turning once, until golden. Leave to cool then roughly chop.

2 Meanwhile, put the tuna in a bowl with the apple, celery and red cabbage.

3 To make the dressing, mix together all the ingredients and season. Spoon the dressing over the tuna mixture and toss until mixed together. Stir in the toasted walnuts.

4 Warm the pitta bread briefly in a toaster then make a slit along one side and open out. Line each pitta with a lettuce leaf and spoon in the tuna mixture. Serve immediately or wrap up and take to work.

Try this Instead of tuna, add 100 g (3½ oz) skinless boneless chicken breast, grilled and sliced.

V For a vegetarian alternative, omit the tuna, dice 50 g (1¾ oz) half fat mature Cheddar cheese and add to the filling in step 2.

Easy freezing...

To preserve its freshness, pitta bread can be stored in the freezer. Then when you're ready to use it, simply take out the number of pitta breads you need and reheat them from frozen in a toaster or under a grill. It's so easy and very convenient.

Mozzarella, tomato and ham quesadilla

Calories per serving 306

Takes 15 mins

Serves 2

calorie controlled cooking spray
2 large low fat tortillas (about 19 cm/ 7½ inches in diameter)
50 g (1¾ oz) lean ham
100 g (3½ oz) light mozzarella cheese, sliced
1 tomato, sliced into rounds
6 large fresh basil leaves
freshly ground black pepper

This toasted tortilla sandwich is delicious cut into wedges and served warm or cold with vegetable crudités.

1 Spray a large non stick frying pan with the cooking spray.

2 Place one of the tortillas in the pan and top with the ham, mozzarella, tomato and basil. Season with black pepper and top with the second tortilla, gently pressing the top down and the edges together.

3 Put the pan over a medium heat, and cook the quesadilla for about 4 minutes until the base is golden and the mozzarella is starting to melt. Remove the pan from the heat, place a serving plate over the pan and carefully flip the quesadilla out on to the plate.

4 Spray the pan again then slide the quesadilla into the pan. Cook for another 4 minutes, turning the heat down slightly if the tortilla is cooking too quickly, until the tortilla is golden. Slide the quesadilla on to a plate and leave to cool slightly before cutting into quarters.

(V) Try this For a vegetarian version, replace the ham with 4 tablespoons of canned black beans, drained and rinsed. Mash the beans slightly with the back of a fork before spooning them on top of the mozzarella in step 2.

Creamy tomato and lentil soup

Calories per serving 145

20 mins prep, 30 mins cooking

(V) (❄)

Serves 4

1 large onion, chopped finely
calorie controlled cooking spray
1 carrot, peeled and sliced
1 celery stick, sliced
100 g (3½ oz) dried split red lentils
1 litre (1¾ pints) vegetable stock
2 bay leaves
2 long fresh rosemary sprigs
500 ml (18 fl oz) passata
4 teaspoons half fat crème fraîche
salt and freshly ground black pepper

Enjoy this filling soup with a medium slice of wholemeal bread per person.

1 Put the onion in a large, lidded, non stick saucepan and then spray with the cooking spray. Cover and sauté over a medium heat for 6 minutes, stirring regularly. Add a splash of water if they start to stick. Add the carrot and celery, spray again with the cooking spray, and cook, covered, for another 2 minutes.

2 Stir in the lentils and add the stock, bay leaves and rosemary. Bring up to the boil then stir, reduce the heat, and simmer for 20 minutes, skimming off any froth that rises to the surface.

3 Remove the rosemary sprigs and bay leaves. Add the passata and cook for another 8–10 minutes, stirring occasionally. Season to taste and stir in (or drizzle over) the crème fraîche before serving.

Couscous salad with sausage and nectarine

Calories per serving 353

Takes 25 mins

Serves 2

90 g (3¼ oz) dried couscous
125 ml (4 fl oz) boiling water
½ vegetable stock cube
calorie controlled cooking spray
3 x 50 g (1¾ oz) reduced fat pork sausages
1 teaspoon cumin seeds
2 garlic cloves, chopped finely
½ teaspoon dried chilli flakes
1 teaspoon ground coriander
juice of ½ a lemon
2 tablespoons chopped fresh coriander
2 tablespoons chopped fresh parsley
a large handful of watercress
1 nectarine, stoned and diced

This salad can be made a day in advance but don't top it with the nectarine until just before serving to preserve its freshness.

1 Pour the couscous into a bowl, cover with the boiling water, crumble in the stock cube and stir. Cover with a plate and set aside for 6–8 minutes until the stock is absorbed.

2 Meanwhile, heat a non stick frying pan, spray with the cooking spray and cook the sausages for about 8 minutes, turning occasionally. Remove from the pan and set aside to cool slightly, then cut each into four pieces.

3 Spray the pan again, add the cumin seeds, garlic and chilli and stir fry for a minute. Remove from the heat and stir in the couscous, coriander, lemon juice, fresh herbs and sausages.

4 Serve the couscous on a bed of watercress, topped with the nectarine.

(V) Try this Swap the pork sausages for vegetarian sausages.

Bacon, lentil and mustard salad

Calories per serving 293

Takes 15 mins

Serves 1

calorie controlled cooking spray
3 lean smoked bacon medallions, about 60 g (2 oz)
1 celery stick, chopped finely
2 spring onions, sliced
140 g (5 oz) canned green lentils, drained and rinsed
4 cherry tomatoes, halved
1 tablespoon chopped fresh parsley, to garnish
For the dressing
1 tablespoon lemon juice
1 tablespoon wholegrain mustard
1 small garlic clove, crushed
freshly ground black pepper

Canned lentils and beans make great storecupboard staples. This substantial salad requires little in the way of accompaniments and can be served warm or at room temperature.

1 Heat a large non stick frying pan, spray with the cooking spray and add the bacon. Cook for about 6 minutes until golden, turning once. Remove the bacon from the pan and cut into bite size pieces.

2 Put the celery, spring onions, lentils, tomatoes and bacon in a bowl. Mix together the lemon juice, mustard and garlic then season with black pepper. Pour the dressing over the lentils then toss until everything is coated. Sprinkle with the parsley before serving.

(V) Try this For a vegetarian alternative, omit the bacon and top the salad with a hard boiled egg, halved.

Souffléd cheese on toast

Calories per serving 195

Takes 15 mins

Serves 2

2 medium slices wholemeal bread
1 egg, separated
1 teaspoon wholegrain mustard
4 dashes of Worcestershire sauce
40 g (1½ oz) half fat mature Cheddar cheese, grated
salt and freshly ground black pepper
For the salad
5 large round lettuce leaves, torn
a handful of rocket leaves
2 teaspoons lemon juice
6 cherry tomatoes, halved
1 tablespoon snipped fresh chives

The egg gives a light, fluffy texture to this scrumptious cheese on toast.

1 Preheat the grill to medium-high and line the grill pan with foil. Lightly toast one side of each slice of bread.

2 Meanwhile, whisk the egg white in a bowl until it forms soft peaks. In a separate bowl, combine the egg yolk, mustard, Worcestershire sauce and cheese. Season and then fold into the egg white.

3 Remove the toast from the grill and spoon the cheese mixture on top of the ungrilled side, dividing it equally between the two slices. Return the toast to the grill and cook for 2 minutes or until the cheese has risen and is golden.

4 Toss the lettuce and rocket in the lemon juice and top with the tomatoes and chives, season and serve with the cheese toasts.

Lamb and rice salad with cumin dressing

Calories per serving 441

Takes 15 mins

Serves 1

1 teaspoon flaked almonds
110 g (4 oz) cooked brown basmati rice
1 tablespoon raisins
1 small carrot, peeled and grated
2 radishes, sliced
75 g (2¾ oz) cooked lean lamb, sliced into strips
a small handful of rocket leaves
For the dressing
1 teaspoon olive oil
1 tablespoon lemon juice
¼ teaspoon ground cumin
¼ teaspoon dried chilli flakes (optional)
salt and freshly ground black pepper

Leftover rice can be put to good use in this lightly spiced salad. Keep the leftover rice refrigerated and make sure it's cool before you use it.

1 Put the flaked almonds in a dry non stick frying pan and toast over a medium-low heat, tossing occasionally, for 3 minutes or until light golden. Remove from the pan and leave to cool.

2 To make the dressing, mix together all the ingredients in a small bowl then season to taste.

3 Put the rice in a salad bowl with the raisins, carrot, radishes, and almonds. Pour the dressing over and toss until mixed together. Top with the cooked lamb and rocket leaves.

V **Try this** For a vegetarian alternative, omit the lamb and crumble over 25 g (1 oz) light feta cheese instead.

Cook's tip If cooking the rice from scratch, cook 45 g (1½ oz) dried brown basmati rice, following the instructions on page 112 for Perfectly Cooked Rice, and leave to cool.

Sesame beef noodles

Calories per serving 192

Takes 15 mins

Serves 2

75 g (2¾ oz) dried medium egg noodles
75 g (2¾ oz) sugar snap peas, sliced diagonally
½ red pepper, de-seeded and cut into thin strips
1 carrot, peeled and cut into thin sticks
1 spring onion, shredded
125 g (4½ oz) cooked thickly sliced beef, diced
4 small sprigs of fresh coriander
For the dressing
1 teaspoon toasted sesame oil
2 tablespoons light soy sauce
1 teaspoon finely chopped fresh root ginger
freshly ground black pepper

To save time, prepare the noodles in advance and dress them in the soy sauce and sesame oil to prevent them from drying out. Then all you need to do on the day is stir in the vegetables, fresh herbs and ginger.

1 Bring a saucepan of water to the boil, add the noodles and cook for about 4 minutes or until tender, then drain and refresh under cold running water. Drain again.

2 Put the noodles in a bowl with the sugar snap peas, red pepper, carrot, spring onion and beef.

3 To make the dressing, mix together all the ingredients and season with black pepper.

4 Pour the dressing over the noodles and toss until everything is coated. Stir in the coriander leaves and serve.

V Try this For a vegetarian alternative, swap the beef for the same weight of marinated tofu pieces. Spray with cooking spray and stir fry for 5 minutes. Leave to cool before adding to the salad in step 2.

Love leftovers...

This noodle dish is ideal for using up any leftovers from the Sunday roast: 125 g (4½ oz) of chicken, turkey or pork would all work equally well.

Chinese noodle soup

Calories per serving 238

Takes 15 mins

(V) **Serves 1**

50 g (1¾ oz) dried wholemeal noodles
¼ red pepper, de-seeded and sliced into
    thin strips
1 small carrot, peeled and cut into matchsticks
1 teaspoon finely chopped fresh root ginger
1 spring onion, sliced diagonally
½ a kettleful of boiling water
1 sachet (8 g) instant miso soup
1 teaspoon soy sauce
¼ teaspoon sesame oil
a few fresh coriander leaves
a large pinch of dried chilli flakes (optional)

Miso is made from soya beans and can be found in supermarkets in a paste or powder form. Either is fine for this recipe but look out for the useful individual sachets.

1 Bring a saucepan of water to the boil then add the noodles. Cook for 3–5 minutes until tender, then drain and put in a serving bowl.

2 Top the noodles with the red pepper, carrot, ginger and half of the spring onion. Pour 250 ml (9 fl oz) just boiled water into a mug and stir in the sachet of miso soup with the soy sauce and sesame oil. When the miso has dissolved, pour it over the noodles and vegetables.

3 Sprinkle the remaining spring onion, coriander and chilli flakes, if using, over the top and serve.

Cook's tip You can prepare the soup in advance and put it in a soup flask to take to work. Warm the flask first by filling it with just boiled water. After 10–15 minutes, pour away the water and fill with the soup; this will help to keep it warm until lunchtime. If you don't have a flask, cook the noodles and prepare the other ingredients in advance then make the sachet of miso soup at lunchtime and simply pour it over the prepared ingredients.

Smoked mackerel and potato salad

Calories per serving 349

Takes 15 mins

Serves 2

200 g (7 oz) new potatoes, scrubbed and halved
    or quartered, if large
140 g (5 oz) smoked mackerel
40 g (1½ oz) fennel, trimmed and sliced thinly
5 cm (2 inch) cucumber, quartered, de-seeded
    and sliced
40 g (1½ oz) watercress, trimmed
1 tablespoon chopped fresh dill
½ teaspoon fine strips of lemon zest (optional)
For the dressing
3 tablespoons Quark
1 teaspoon lemon juice
1 teaspoon tartare sauce
freshly ground black pepper

This salad makes a complete, filling lunch and is ideal to take to work. Simply store in the fridge until ready to eat.

1 Bring a saucepan of water to the boil, add the potatoes and cook for about 10 minutes until tender. Drain then leave to cool.

2 Meanwhile, mix together the ingredients for the dressing, adding 1 teaspoon of water, then season to taste with black pepper.

3 Flake the mackerel into large chunks, removing any bones. Put the potatoes in a large bowl with the mackerel, fennel and cucumber.

4 Pour the dressing over the salad and toss until coated. Line two containers or plates with the watercress then spoon the mackerel salad on top. Scatter over the dill and lemon zest, if using.

Piperade wrap

Calories per serving 338

Takes 15 mins

(V) **Serves 1**

calorie controlled cooking spray
25 g (1 oz) red pepper, de-seeded and diced
1 spring onion, sliced thinly
1 tomato, de-seeded and diced
2 small eggs, beaten lightly
1 large low fat tortilla wrap (about 19 cm /
    7½ inches in diameter)
salt and freshly ground black pepper

Piperade comes from the Basque region of France and it's a lovely way to jazz up scrambled eggs.

1 Heat a small, heavy based, non stick pan and spray with the cooking spray. Add the red pepper, spring onion and tomato and stir fry for 2 minutes until softened.

2 Pour in the eggs, season, and cook, stirring constantly to prevent the eggs from sticking, until scrambled.

3 Meanwhile, heat a large frying pan and warm the tortilla for about 2 minutes, turning once. This helps to soften the tortilla.

4 Spoon the piperade on to one half of the warm tortilla, tuck in the ends and roll up. Slice in half on the diagonal.

TLT on toast

Calories per serving 159

Takes 10 mins

Serves 1

2 x 25 g (1 oz) turkey rashers
1 medium slice granary bread
2 teaspoons extra light mayonnaise
½ garlic clove, crushed
1 teaspoon lemon juice
2 round lettuce leaves
4 thin slices of cucumber
1 tomato, diced
freshly ground black pepper

This twist on the classic BLT is made with crisp rashers of grilled turkey instead of bacon and is served on top of lightly toasted granary bread, spread with a garlicky lemon mayonnaise.

1 Preheat the grill to high and line the grill pan with foil. Grill the turkey rashers for 2 minutes on each side. At the same time, lightly toast both sides of the granary bread.

2 Meanwhile, mix together the mayonnaise, garlic and lemon juice and spread it over one side of the toast. Top with the lettuce leaves and cucumber, followed by the turkey rashers and tomato. Season with black pepper before serving.

Cook's tip If you want to enjoy this sandwich as a packed lunch, serve the filling between two medium slices of untoasted granary or wholegrain bread.

Vegetarian

Paella stuffed tomatoes on page 42

Choose from a great selection of tasty recipes for meat-free salads, curries, sausages, and more. Recipes such as the Indonesian Soup with Paneer and Lemongrass and Ginger Tofu Fritters are inspired by the exotic tastes of world cuisine while others, such as the Leek, Apple and Cheese Sausages, bring you the more traditional flavours of home.

Indonesian soup with paneer

Calories per serving 354

Takes 35 mins

(V) **Serves 2**

100 g (3½ oz) dried wholewheat noodles
1 egg
1 large shallot, chopped roughly
2 garlic cloves
25 g (1 oz) fresh root ginger, chopped roughly
calorie controlled cooking spray
1 large lemongrass stalk, outer leaves
     removed and chopped finely
2 dried kaffir lime leaves
600 ml (20 fl oz) vegetable stock
1 teaspoon ground turmeric
4 baby corn, halved lengthways
100 g (3½ oz) sugar snap peas
60 g (2 oz) paneer, cut into 3 slices, then halved
7 cherry tomatoes, halved
25 g (1 oz) beansprouts
leaves from 2 fresh coriander sprigs
salt and freshly ground black pepper

Although this aromatic soup has lots of ingredients, it's very easy to make.

1 Bring a saucepan of water to the boil, add the noodles and cook for 3–5 minutes until tender. Drain and refresh under cold running water. Set aside.

2 Bring a saucepan of water to the boil again, add the egg and cook for 6 minutes. Put the cooked egg in a bowl of cold water to cool, then peel and cut in half.

3 Meanwhile, put the shallot, garlic and ginger in a food processor, or blender, and whizz to a coarse paste. Spray a large saucepan with the cooking spray, add the paste and cook, stirring, for a minute then add the lemongrass and lime leaves.

4 Pour in the stock and bring up to the boil then reduce the heat and simmer for 5 minutes. Add the turmeric, baby corn and sugar snap peas and simmer for a further 3 minutes. Season to taste.

5 Meanwhile, heat a non stick frying pan, spray with the cooking spray and fry the paneer for 2–3 minutes, turning halfway, until golden.

6 Divide the noodles between two large shallow bowls and add the tomatoes and beansprouts. Pour the broth over and top each bowl with the coriander leaves, half an egg and some crisp paneer. Serve immediately.

Something different...

Paneer is a popular Indian cheese – you'll find it in the chiller cabinet in many supermarkets or in oriental shops. It can be cooked until crisp or simply stirred into curries.

Mushrooms with white bean mash

Calories per serving 239

Takes 30 mins

(V)

Serves 2

½ red pepper, de-seeded and cut into 1 cm (½ inch) long slices
2 large portobello mushrooms, stalks removed
calorie controlled cooking spray
1 teaspoon cumin seeds
1 teaspoon olive oil
2 large garlic cloves, chopped
2.5 cm (1 inch) fresh root ginger, grated
125 g (4½ oz) canned butterbeans, drained and rinsed
50 ml (2 fl oz) skimmed milk
2 tablespoons lemon juice
85 g (3 oz) light halloumi cheese, cut into two long slices
salt and freshly ground black pepper

1 Preheat the grill to high and line the grill pan with foil. Place the peppers and mushrooms, gill-side up, on the foil. Spray with the cooking spray and grill for 4–5 minutes. Turn everything over, spray again, and grill for another 4–5 minutes until tender and the pepper is charred in places.

2 Meanwhile, toast the cumin seeds in a dry non stick saucepan for 2 minutes then add the olive oil, garlic and ginger to the pan and cook for a minute. Add the butterbeans and cook for about 5 minutes, stirring, adding a splash of water if they start to stick.

3 Pour in the milk and warm through then mash to a coarse purée. Stir in the lemon juice and season.

4 Heat a griddle or non stick frying pan until hot and spray the halloumi with the cooking spray. Cook the halloumi for about 2–3 minutes on each side until golden.

5 Reheat the bean mash and spoon it on top of the mushrooms. Top with a slice of halloumi and red pepper. Season then serve.

Try this Replace the halloumi with a rasher of lean back bacon per person, grilled until crisp.

Eggah

Calories per serving 238

Takes 30 mins

(V)

Serves 4

250 g (9 oz) sweet potato, peeled and cut into 1 cm (½ inch) dice
calorie controlled cooking spray
1 onion, halved and sliced
1 small red pepper, de-seeded and diced
1 courgette, diced
1 red chilli, de-seeded and sliced thinly (optional)
2 garlic cloves, chopped finely
1 teaspoon cumin seeds
1 teaspoon ground coriander
6 eggs, beaten lightly
8 cherry tomatoes
salt and freshly ground black pepper

This Middle Eastern version of a Spanish tortilla is delicious with the Tomato, Red Onion and Mint Salad (see page 108).

1 Bring a saucepan of water to the boil, add the potato and cook for about 8 minutes until tender. Drain.

2 Meanwhile, heat a large, lidded, grill proof, non stick frying pan (see Cook's tip). Spray with the cooking spray and cook the onion, covered, for 6 minutes, stirring occasionally. Add the pepper and courgette, spray again, and cook for another 5 minutes.

3 Preheat the grill to medium-high. Stir in the chilli, garlic and cumin and cook for 2 minutes, then add the coriander and potato. Spread the mixture in an even layer over the base of the pan and pour over the eggs, season, and arrange the cherry tomatoes over the top.

4 Cook over a medium-low heat for 6 minutes until the base is set and golden then transfer the pan to the grill and cook for a further 5–6 minutes until just set. Serve cut into four wedges.

Cook's tip If your frying pan isn't grill proof, wrap the handle in foil before you put it under the grill.

Aubergine, lemon and bean stew

Calories per serving 128

30 mins prep, 15 mins cooking

Ⓥ ✳

Serves 4

1 aubergine, cut into large bite size pieces
2 large garlic cloves
1 teaspoon cumin seeds
1 teaspoon fennel seeds
500 g (1 lb 2 oz) passata
1 tablespoon tomato purée
juice and grated zest of 1 small lemon
400 g can butterbeans, drained and rinsed
50 g (1¾ oz) pitted black olives in brine,
    drained and rinsed
salt and freshly ground black pepper

You might like to try this with 50 g (1¾ oz) dried couscous per person.

1 Bring about 2.5 cm (1 inch) water to the boil in a lidded saucepan. Put the aubergine and garlic in a steamer basket placed over the water, cover and steam for 8 minutes until softened. Alternatively, bring about 1 cm (½ inch) of water to the boil in a lidded pan, add the aubergine and garlic and cook until tender.

2 Meanwhile, toast the cumin and fennel seeds in a lidded non stick saucepan for about 2 minutes until they release their aromas. Add the passata, tomato purée, 4 tablespoons of water and the lemon juice.

3 Using a fork, roughly mash the aubergine and garlic together then add to the pan along with the passata, butterbeans and olives.

4 Bring up to the boil, then reduce the heat, partially cover the saucepan, and simmer for 15 minutes until thickened and reduced. Season to taste then serve sprinkled with the lemon zest.

Home style vegetarian curry

Calories per serving 245

30 mins prep, 30 mins cooking

Ⓥ ✳

Serves 2

calorie controlled cooking spray
1 onion, sliced thinly
3 garlic cloves, chopped finely
40 g (1½ oz) fresh root ginger, chopped finely
2 teaspoons ground cumin
2 teaspoons ground coriander
5 cardamom pods, split
2 bay leaves
2 curry leaf sprigs
200 g (7 oz) sweet potatoes, peeled and cut into
    1 cm (½ inch) chunks
½ red chilli, de-seeded and chopped
250 ml (9 fl oz) vegetable stock
200 g (7 oz) canned chopped tomatoes
125 g (4½ oz) small cauliflower florets
1 carrot, peeled and sliced
75 g (2¾ oz) spring greens, shredded
1 teaspoon lemon juice
1 tablespoon chopped fresh coriander

Serve this aromatic curry with 40 g (1½ oz) dried basmati rice per person, cooked according to the packet instructions.

1 Heat a large, lidded, non stick saucepan and spray with the cooking spray. Cook the onion, covered, for 10 minutes, adding a splash of water if they start to stick. Add the garlic and three quarters of the ginger and cook for another 2 minutes then stir in the spices, bay and curry leaf sprigs, sweet potatoes and chilli.

2 Add the stock and tomatoes, stir, and bring up to the boil. Reduce the heat and simmer for 10 minutes, covered, then add the cauliflower and carrot. Simmer, partially covered, for another 15 minutes until the vegetables are tender.

3 Add the spring greens and lemon juice then cook, uncovered, for a further 5 minutes. Remove the bay leaves and curry leaf sprigs, and serve sprinkled with coriander and the remaining ginger.

Try this If preferred, replace the fresh spices with 2 tablespoons of balti curry paste.

Lemongrass and ginger tofu fritters

Calories per serving 172

Takes 20 mins

(V) **(❋)**   **Serves 4**

285 g (10 oz) firm tofu, patted dry with kitchen
    towels and grated coarsely
3 garlic cloves, chopped finely
1 red chilli, de-seeded and chopped finely
2 lemongrass stalks, outer leaves removed and
    chopped finely
2.5 cm (1 inch) piece fresh root ginger, grated
3 spring onions, chopped finely
3 tablespoons chopped fresh coriander, plus extra
    to garnish
1 tablespoon light soy sauce
1 egg white
3 tablespoons plain flour
calorie controlled cooking spray
freshly ground black pepper
4 lime wedges, to serve
For the chilli dipping sauce
2 tablespoons extra light mayonnaise
2 tablespoons sweet chilli sauce
1 tablespoon lime juice

Lemongrass, red chilli, garlic and ginger give these fritters a fabulous
Thai flavour. Serve them on a bed of lettuce leaves with grated carrots
and chopped chilli.

1 Squeeze the tofu in your hands to remove all excess water (this is
important to ensure the mixture holds together well). Put the tofu in a
mixing bowl with the garlic, chilli, lemongrass, ginger, spring onions,
coriander, soy sauce, egg white and flour. Season with black pepper and
stir until combined.

2 Form the mixture into eight patties.

3 Meanwhile, mix together all the ingredients for the chilli dipping sauce
in a bowl and set aside.

4 Heat a large non stick frying pan, spray with the cooking spray and
cook the fritters, four at a time, for 4–5 minutes on each side until golden.
Serve two patties per person with a spoonful of the dipping sauce and
lime wedges for squeezing over.

A good start...

These delicious fritters would make a good starter before the
Roasted Lemongrass Chicken on page 100.

Indian salad with flaked almonds

Calories per serving 336

Takes 35 mins

(V)   **Serves 1**

100 g (3½ oz) new potatoes, scrubbed and halved
125 g (4½ oz) small cauliflower florets
15 g (½ oz) flaked almonds
50 g (1¾ oz) canned chick peas, drained and rinsed
1 tablespoon chopped red onion
1 tomato, de-seeded and chopped
1 tablespoon chopped fresh coriander
For the dressing
1 tablespoon tamarind paste
2 tablespoons plain low fat yogurt
1 tablespoon finely chopped fresh root ginger
1 tablespoon lemon juice
a large pinch of ground cumin
salt and freshly ground black pepper

A fun way to serve this salad is on top of a crisp poppadum.

1 Bring a saucepan of water to the boil, add the potatoes and cook for 10 minutes or until tender. Drain then cut into bite size pieces.

2 Meanwhile, put the cauliflower in a steamer basket placed over a saucepan of 2.5 cm (1 inch) of gently boiling water and cook for 3–5 minutes until just tender. Alternatively, if you don't have a steamer basket, bring a pan of water to the boil, add the cauliflower and cook until just tender.

3 Put the almonds in a dry non stick frying pan and toast over a medium-low heat for 2–3 minutes until light golden. Remove from the heat and leave to cool.

4 Mix together the ingredients for the dressing with 1 tablespoon of hot water and season.

5 Combine the potatoes, cauliflower and chick peas in a bowl then spoon the dressing over. Toss until coated then spoon on to a serving plate. Top with the red onion, tomato, coriander and flaked almonds. Serve immediately.

(V) Try this You can add 100 g (3½ oz) cooked, diced Quorn to the salad in step 4.

Did you know?

> Tamarind is available as a paste or in a powdered or concentrated form. It's widely used in Asian and Middle Eastern food and gives a slightly sour flavour to curries, chutneys and soups. It is also a key ingredient in Worcestershire sauce.

Leek, apple and cheese sausages

Calories per serving 232

20 mins prep + 30 mins chilling, 14 mins cooking

V ❄

Serves 4

150 g (5½ oz) fresh white breadcrumbs
100 g (3½ oz) half fat mature Cheddar cheese
1 small leek, chopped very finely
1 small green apple, unpeeled and grated
1 teaspoon dried thyme
2 eggs
1 teaspoon Dijon mustard
calorie controlled cooking spray
salt and freshly ground black pepper

These sausages are delicious with the Cauliflower Mash (see page 106) and 50 g (1¾ oz) green beans per person.

1 In a large bowl, mix together 100 g (3½ oz) of the breadcrumbs with the cheese, leek, apple and thyme. Lightly beat one of the eggs and stir into the breadcrumb mixture with the mustard, then season.

2 Divide the mixture into eight and form each one into a sausage shape. Chill for 30 minutes to firm up. Preheat the grill to high and line the grill pan with foil.

3 Beat the second egg in a shallow dish. Dip each sausage into the egg, and then the remaining breadcrumbs, and place on the foil. Spray with the cooking spray then grill for 12–14 minutes, turning halfway and spraying again, until golden and crisp on the outside. Serve two sausages per person.

V **Try this** Add a watercress sauce. Mix 2 tablespoons fat free fromage frais with 1 tablespoon lemon juice, 1 teaspoon finely grated lemon zest and 75 g (2¾ oz) watercress, tough stalks removed and leaves chopped finely. Season to taste.

Asian Quorn and pineapple salad

Calories per serving 249

Takes 35 mins

V

Serves 1

2 x 55 g (2¾ oz) frozen Quorn fillets
2 tablespoons hoisin sauce
calorie controlled cooking spray
40 g (1½ oz) rocket leaves
75 g (2¾ oz) canned diced pineapple in natural juice, drained
2 radishes, sliced into rounds
1 tablespoon chopped red onion
2.5 cm (1 inch) cucumber, de-seeded and diced
1 heaped tablespoon chopped fresh mint
For the dressing
1 teaspoon light soy sauce
a large pinch of dried chilli flakes
1 teaspoon caster sugar
1 tablespoon lime juice

Serve this fragrant salad with a mini naan bread.

1 Preheat the oven to Gas Mark 6/200°C/fan oven 180°C. Put the Quorn fillets in a dish and spoon the hoisin sauce over both sides.

2 Spray a non stick baking tray with the cooking spray and add the Quorn. Cook for about 25 minutes, turning after 12 minutes, spooning over the hoisin sauce until golden and cooked through.

3 Meanwhile, mix together the ingredients for the dressing. Place the rocket on a serving plate and top with the pineapple, radishes, onion and cucumber. Spoon over three quarters of the dressing.

4 Slice the Quorn fillets on the diagonal and arrange on top of the salad. Drizzle the remaining dressing over the Quorn then top with the mint before serving.

Try this Swap the Quorn for 175 g (6 oz) skinless boneless chicken breast. Prepare and cook in the same way.

Yellow pea and tofu curry

Calories per serving 320

20 mins prep + 30 mins marinating,

40 mins cooking

(V) (✳) curry only   **Serves 4**

2 tablespoons balti curry paste
2 tablespoons lime juice
250 g (9 oz) firm tofu, patted dry and cut into
        8 long slices
200 g (7 oz) dried yellow split peas
calorie controlled cooking spray
1 large onion, chopped
30 g (1¼ oz) fresh root ginger, grated
1 teaspoon cumin seeds
1 teaspoon mustard seeds
1 teaspoon ground turmeric
2 teaspoons ground coriander
1 large red chilli, halved lengthways
2 carrots, peeled and diced
300 ml (10 fl oz) vegetable stock
100 ml (3½ fl oz) light coconut milk
salt and freshly ground black pepper
a few fresh coriander sprigs, to garnish

Yellow split peas make an economical and filling curry. They're easy to use too since they don't need to be pre-soaked. The tofu is marinated in spices then served on top of the curry. Serve with a warmed 42 g wholemeal chapati per person.

1 Mix together the curry paste and lime juice with 1 tablespoon of warm water, then season. Add the tofu, turn to coat it, then leave to marinate for 30 minutes.

2 Put the split peas in a colander and rinse under cold running water then tip into a medium lidded saucepan, cover with plenty of water and bring up to the boil. Reduce the heat, partially cover the pan, and simmer for 40 minutes until tender. Skim off any foam that rises to the surface, topping up with more water if necessary. Drain the peas then set aside.

3 Meanwhile, preheat the oven to Gas Mark 4/180°C/fan oven 160°C. Spray a large, lidded, non stick saucepan with the cooking spray and cook the onion gently for 10 minutes, adding a splash of water if they start to stick, until softened and golden. Stir in the ginger and spices and cook for another minute.

4 Spray a roasting tin with the cooking spray then roast the tofu for 20 minutes, turning halfway.

5 Tip the peas into the large saucepan with the chilli, carrots and stock. Season and bring up to the boil then reduce the heat and simmer for 15 minutes, partially covered, until the vegetables are tender, then stir in the coconut milk and half of the fresh coriander. Simmer, partially covered, for another 5 minutes until warmed through.

6 Serve the curry in shallow bowls with the tofu on top and sprinkled with the remaining coriander.

Make it speedy...

> To save time, you could use split red lentils instead of split peas. They cook in half the time so you only need to simmer them for 20 minutes in step 2. You can then continue with the recipe from this point.

Linguine with broad beans and rocket

Calories per serving 335

Takes 20 mins

(V)   **Serves 1**

60 g (2 oz) shelled broad beans, defrosted if frozen
60 g (2 oz) dried linguine
calorie controlled cooking spray
1 garlic clove, chopped finely
2 tablespoons low fat soft cheese
1 tablespoon lemon juice
25 g (1 oz) rocket leaves
salt and freshly ground black pepper

1 Bring a saucepan of water to the boil, add the broad beans and cook for 2 minutes then refresh under cold water. When cool, slip them out of their grey outer shell to reveal a bright green bean inside.

2 Meanwhile, bring another saucepan of water to the boil, add the pasta and cook, following the packet instructions, until al dente. Drain, reserving 2 tablespoons of the cooking water.

3 Heat a non stick frying pan and spray with the cooking spray. Cook the garlic for 1 minute then stir in the soft cheese, lemon juice and reserved pasta cooking water. Add the pasta and broad beans, toss until combined and warmed through.

4 Remove from the heat and stir in the rocket and season before serving.

Paella stuffed tomatoes

Calories per serving 257

Takes 50 mins

(V)   **Serves 2**

2 large beefsteak tomatoes
40 g (1½ oz) shelled broad beans, defrosted if
    frozen
calorie controlled cooking spray
1 onion, chopped finely
2 garlic cloves, chopped
½ red pepper, de-seeded and diced
½ teaspoon smoked paprika
½ teaspoon turmeric
60 g (2 oz) paella rice
150 ml (5 fl oz) vegetable stock
40 g (1½ oz) pitted black olives, chopped
2 teaspoons flaked toasted almonds
salt and freshly ground black pepper
a handful of fresh basil leaves, to garnish

1 Slice the top off each tomato to make a lid and set aside. Using a teaspoon, scoop out the centre, leaving a shell. Sprinkle the inside with salt, turn upside down and leave to drain for 30 minutes. Rinse the inside of the tomatoes then drain again.

2 Meanwhile, bring a saucepan of water to the boil, add the broad beans and cook for 2–3 minutes until tender. Drain and refresh under cold water then, when cool, slip the beans out of their grey jackets. Set aside.

3 Heat a deep sided, lidded, non stick frying pan. Spray with the cooking spray, add the onion and cook, covered, for 6 minutes, stirring regularly until softened. Stir in the garlic and red pepper, cover and cook for another 3 minutes.

4 Preheat the oven to Gas Mark 4/180°C/fan oven 160°C. Add the spices and rice to the pan then stir until combined. Pour in the stock, bring to the boil, stir, then reduce the heat to its lowest setting. Simmer, covered, for 15 minutes without stirring, until the stock is absorbed. Stir the olives and broad beans into the rice.

5 Spray a small baking dish with the cooking spray, spoon the paella into the tomatoes, pressing it down slightly, and top with the lid. Spray the tomatoes with the cooking spray then roast for 15 minutes or until the tomatoes are softened. Serve one tomato per person topped with the toasted almonds and garnished with basil.

Try this For a seafood paella, omit the broad beans and stir 175 g (6 oz) frozen cooked and peeled prawns into the rice in step 4. Heat through for 2 minutes before stuffing the tomatoes.

Thai fried rice with toasted cashews

Calories per serving 274

Takes 35 mins

(V)   **Serves 1**

50 g (1¾ oz) dried Thai jasmine rice
calorie controlled cooking spray
1 cm (½ inch) piece fresh root ginger, cut into very
      thin strips
6 cashew nuts
1 teaspoon soy sauce
2 spring onions, sliced diagonally
1 garlic clove, chopped
1 lemongrass stalk, peeled and chopped finely
½ red chilli, de-seeded and chopped
2 fresh coriander sprigs, leaves only
For the dressing
1 tablespoon soy sauce
1 teaspoon lime juice
a large pinch of caster sugar

For the best results, make sure the cooked rice is completely cold before stir frying, and piping hot before serving. Serve with sugar snap peas.

1 Put the rice in a lidded pan and pour in enough cold water to cover by 1 cm (½ inch). Bring up to the boil then reduce the heat to its lowest setting. Cover and simmer for about 10 minutes until the rice is tender and the water is absorbed. Remove from the heat. Leave to stand for 5 minutes, still covered. Spread the rice out on a baking tray. Leave to cool.

2 Heat a non stick wok or frying pan then spray with the cooking spray. Add the ginger and stir fry for 3 minutes until it becomes crisp and golden. Remove from the pan and set aside.

3 Put the cashew nuts in the pan, spray with the cooking spray and toast over a medium-low heat for 2 minutes, turning them frequently. Add the soy sauce and turn to coat the nuts, cook for another minute until golden then remove from the pan and set aside.

4 Wipe the pan, spray with the cooking spray then stir fry the white part of the spring onions, garlic, lemongrass and chilli for a minute. Add the cold rice, turn it to break up any lumps and combine with the other ingredients.

5 Mix together the soy sauce, lime juice and sugar. Pour the mixture into the pan, stir and heat through. Stir the green part of the spring onion into the rice. Serve topped with the coriander, cashews nuts and crisp ginger.

Before you start...

Because a stir fry cooks very quickly, it's best to prepare all the ingredients in advance so you have them to hand and everything runs smoothly.

Veggie stew with dumplings

Calories per serving 362

35 mins prep, 20 mins cooking

Ⓥ ❋   **Serves 2**

calorie controlled cooking spray
1 onion, sliced
1 celery stick, sliced
1 leek, sliced
2 turnips, cut into bite size pieces
125 g (4 ½ oz) baby carrots, trimmed and scrubbed
60 g (2 oz) button mushrooms
1 teaspoon plain flour
3 fresh thyme sprigs
1 bay leaf
1 teaspoon strong coffee granules, made up
    to 75 ml (3 fl oz)
150 ml (5 fl oz) vegetable stock
1 tablespoon dark soy sauce
150 g (5½ oz) canned borlotti beans, rinsed and
    drained
salt and freshly ground black pepper
For the cheese and herb dumplings
40 g (1½ oz) self raising flour
25 g (1 oz) half fat mature Cheddar cheese, grated
1 tablespoon chopped fresh sage
25 g (1 oz) low fat spread

With its light and fluffy cheese and herb dumplings, this veggie-packed stew is pure comfort food. Adding coffee to the stock may sound odd but it creates a delicious richness.

1 Heat a lidded casserole dish, spray with the cooking spray add the onion and cook for 6 minutes until softened. Add the celery and leek and cook for another 2 minutes then add the turnips, baby carrots and mushrooms. Stir in the flour and cook for 1 minute, stirring.

2 Add the thyme and bay leaf then pour in the coffee, stock, soy sauce and borlotti beans. Bring up to the boil then reduce the heat and simmer for 10 minutes, stirring occasionally. Season to taste.

3 Meanwhile, make the dumplings. Mix together the flour, cheese, sage and low fat spread in a bowl. Stir in about 1–2 teaspoons water and bring the mixture together with your hands to make a firm ball of dough. Divide the dough into four walnut size pieces and form into dumplings.

4 Arrange the dumplings in the casserole so they are half submerged in the stew. Cover with a lid and simmer over a low heat for 20 minutes until the dumplings have risen and the vegetables are tender.

Get ahead...

Here's the perfect make ahead dish for a delicious midweek meal for two. The stew can be made up to 2 days in advance. Prepare it up to the end of step 3 only and then store, covered, in the fridge. To serve, reheat for 5 minutes, stirring, and then continue from step 4.

Quick & easy

Jerk chicken with Carribean beans on page 54

We're all busy these days so more good ideas for meals-in-minutes are always welcome. With recipes such as Sausage Pizza, Weekday Chicken and 'Chips' or Crispy Potato and Meatball Pan Fry, you'll find what you're looking for in this chapter, whether you're cooking for one or for the whole family.

Sausage pizza

Calories per serving 304

30 mins prep, 15 mins cooking

❄

Serves 4

1 x 145 g pizza base mix
calorie controlled cooking spray
2 tablespoons plain flour, for dusting
175 ml (6 fl oz) passata
1 teaspoon dried oregano
1 tablespoon tomato purée
½ teaspoon dried chilli flakes (optional)
4 reduced fat pork sausages
150 g (5½ oz) light mozzarella cheese, drained
    and torn into pieces
salt and freshly ground black pepper
a small handful of fresh basil leaves, to garnish

1 Prepare the pizza base mix by following the packet instructions. Spray a 25 x 35 cm (10 x 14 inch) baking tray with the cooking spray and dust with a little of the flour. Roll out the pizza dough thinly on a lightly floured work surface to a 30 x 23 cm (12 x 9 inch) rectangle. Transfer to the baking tray and set aside to rest for 10 minutes.

2 Preheat the oven to Gas Mark 7/220°C/fan oven 200°C. Mix together the passata, oregano, tomato purée and chilli flakes, if using. Spoon the sauce over the base in a thin layer, leaving a 1 cm (½ inch) gap around the edge.

3 Squeeze the sausage meat out of their skins and make into 28 marble sized balls and arrange them on the top of the pizza, followed by the mozzarella and seasoning. Spray the top of the pizza with the cooking spray.

4 Bake in the oven for about 12–15 minutes until the base is golden and crisp. Garnish with the basil leaves and cut into four. Serve immediately.

V Try this Swap the pork sausages with 4 vegetarian sausages, sliced thinly.

Turkey balls in crème fraîche sauce

Calories per serving 376

Takes 30 mins

❄

Serves 1

150 g (5½ oz) turkey mince
25 g (1 oz) wholemeal breadcrumbs
15 g (½ oz) Parmesan cheese, grated finely
1 tablespoon snipped fresh chives
2 spring onions, chopped finely
500 ml (18 fl oz) vegetable stock
1½ teaspoons Dijon mustard
1 teaspoon lemon juice
1 tablespoon half fat crème fraîche
40 g (1½ oz) baby spinach leaves
salt and freshly ground black pepper

These meatballs are simple and delicious. Serve with runner beans and a 40 g (1½ oz) slice of crusty bread, for dunking into the sauce.

1 Combine the turkey mince, breadcrumbs, Parmesan cheese, chives and the white part of the spring onions in a bowl. Season well and form into six walnut size balls. Cover and chill until ready to use.

2 Pour the stock into a saucepan and bring up to the boil. Reduce the heat, add the turkey balls and spoon over the stock. Simmer for 4 minutes, turning once, then, using a slotted spoon, remove them from the pan and set aside.

3 Pour away all but 175 ml (6 fl oz) of the stock, add the mustard and lemon juice then bring up to the boil. Turn down the heat and simmer for about 3 minutes until reduced by a third.

4 Stir in the crème fraîche, spinach, half of the green part of the spring onions and the turkey balls. Season and simmer, stirring occasionally, for another 2–3 minutes until the sauce has thickened and the turkey balls are cooked through.

5 Serve the meatballs in a large, shallow bowl, sprinkled with the remaining spring onions.

Halloumi and vegetable burgers

Calories per serving 323

20 mins prep, 25 mins cooking

(V) **Serves 4**

125 g (4½ oz) light halloumi cheese, patted dry
    and grated coarsely
2 carrots, peeled and grated coarsely
125 g (4½ oz) canned sweetcorn, drained
2 large spring onions, chopped
40 g (1½ oz) fresh breadcrumbs
1 egg, beaten lightly
calorie controlled cooking spray
salt and freshly ground black pepper
To serve
4 x 50 g (1¾ oz) wholemeal rolls
4 curly lettuce leaves
tomato slices
red onion slices
cucumber slices
4 tablespoons spicy tomato salsa

Light and juicy, these homemade burgers come with all the trimmings as well as a spoonful of spicy tomato salsa. Serve with 50 g (1¾ oz) reduced calorie coleslaw per person.

1 Put the halloumi, carrot, sweetcorn and spring onions in a food processor and whizz to a coarse paste. Spoon the mixture into a mixing bowl and stir in the breadcrumbs, egg and seasoning. Shape into four burgers – the mixture is quite loose but holds together when cooked.

2 Preheat the oven to Gas Mark 4/180°C/fan oven 160°C and spray a baking tray with the cooking spray. Transfer the burgers to the baking tray, place in the oven and cook for about 20–25 minutes, turning halfway, until cooked through and golden.

3 Meanwhile, cut each roll in half and lightly toast. Top one half of each roll with a lettuce leaf and slices of tomato. Add the burgers and top with cucumber and red onion as well as a tablespoonful of the salsa and finally the top of the roll. Serve straightaway.

Get ahead...

If time allows, you can make these burgers up to a day in advance and then store them, covered, in the fridge until you're ready to cook them. Chilling the burgers firms them up and makes them easier to cook.

Pink trout with pickled cucumber

Calories per serving 236

Takes 30 mins

Serves 1

140 g (5 oz) pink sea trout fillet
salt and freshly ground black pepper
For the pickled cucumber
60 g (2 oz) cucumber, sliced very thinly into rounds
salt
2 teaspoons white wine vinegar
1 teaspoon caster sugar
1 tablespoon chopped fresh dill

Serve this deliciously light and summery dish with 100 g (3½ oz) new potatoes and green beans.

1 To make the pickled cucumber, sprinkle the cucumber with salt then set aside for 15 minutes. Rinse to remove the salt then drain well. Mix together the white wine vinegar, sugar and 2 teaspoons water in a bowl until the sugar dissolves. Add the cucumber and dill then turn until mixed together. Season with black pepper and set aside.

2 Half fill a lidded frying pan with water and bring up to the boil. Place the trout in the pan and return to the boil. Turn off the heat, cover with the lid, and leave the fish to cook in the hot water for 6–8 minutes.

3 Using a fish slice or spatula, remove the trout from the pan and hold it over some kitchen towel to remove excess water. Then place it on a plate with the pickled cucumber. Season to taste before serving.

Jerk chicken with Caribbean beans

Calories per serving 424

Takes 35 mins

bean stew only

Serves 4

8 x 60 g (2 oz) skinless boneless mini chicken fillets
2 tablespoons jerk spice mix
350 g (12 oz) butternut squash, peeled,
      de-seeded, and cut into 1 cm (½ inch) cubes
calorie controlled cooking spray
1 onion, chopped finely
2 large garlic cloves, chopped finely
1 yellow pepper, de-seeded and diced
1 teaspoon dried thyme
1 teaspoon cumin seeds
400 g can black beans, drained and rinsed
3 tablespoons chopped fresh coriander
25 g (1 oz) sweet and hot jalapeños (from a jar),
      drained and chopped roughly
salt and freshly ground black pepper
To serve
4 tortillas
4 tablespoons 0% fat Greek yogurt

1 Put the chicken fillets on a plate. Sprinkle over the jerk spices, coating both sides, then cover and chill. Bring a pan of water to the boil, add the butternut squash and cook for about 10 minutes or until tender. Drain then refresh under cold running water. Set aside.

2 Meanwhile, heat a lidded non stick saucepan, spray with the cooking spray then cook the onion for 8 minutes, covered, stirring regularly. Add the garlic, pepper, thyme and cumin seeds. Spray with cooking spray and fry for another 3 minutes, stirring.

3 Preheat the oven to Gas Mark ¼/110°C/fan oven 90°C. Add the black beans, squash and 2 tablespoons of water to the saucepan with the onions and peppers. Stir and heat through for 5 minutes.

4 While the black bean mixture is cooking, heat a griddle or non stick frying pan, spray the chicken with the cooking spray and cook four of the chicken fillets for 6 minutes, turning once, or until cooked through. When the black beans and squash have finished cooking, season and stir in the coriander and jalapeños.

5 Cover the first batch of cooked chicken and keep warm while you cook the second batch. Meanwhile, wrap the tortillas in foil and warm in the oven. Place a tortilla on each serving plate, top with the black bean mixture then add the chicken. Place a spoonful of yogurt on top before serving.

Weekday chicken and 'chips'

Calories per serving 317

20 mins prep, 30 mins cooking

Serves 2

calorie controlled cooking spray
200 g (7 oz) new potatoes, scrubbed and sliced into
    thin 5 mm (¼ inch) rounds
1 small onion, halved and each half cut into
    4 wedges
2 x 150 g (5½ oz) skinless boneless chicken breasts
6 small bay leaves
1 small red pepper, de-seeded and sliced into
    long strips
6 baby plum tomatoes
2 garlic cloves, unpeeled
a few fresh thyme sprigs
2 tablespoons extra light mayonnaise
½ teaspoon harissa paste
1 teaspoon lemon juice
salt and freshly ground black pepper

Roasted until golden and crisp, the new potato chips and succulent chicken breasts come with a spicy garlic mayonnaise. Serve with broccoli florets and green beans.

1 Preheat the oven to Gas Mark 6/200°C/fan oven 180°C. Spray a 23 x 35 cm (9 x 14 inch) baking dish with the cooking spray. Arrange the potatoes and onion in a single layer in the dish then spray again with the cooking spray. Place in the oven for 5 minutes while you brown the chicken.

2 Heat a non stick frying pan, spray the chicken with the cooking spray and cook over a medium heat for about 5 minutes, turning once, until golden. Remove the chicken from the pan and make three slashes diagonally across the top of each breast. Place a bay leaf in each cut.

3 Remove the roasting dish from the oven, turn the potatoes, and arrange the pepper, plum tomatoes and garlic in the dish, scatter over a few sprigs of thyme then top with the chicken breasts and season.

4 Return the dish to the oven and roast for another 20 minutes then remove the garlic cloves and set aside. Continue to roast the chicken for another 5–10 minutes or until cooked through and the potatoes turn golden and slightly crisp.

5 To make the garlic mayonnaise, squeeze the garlic out of its skin into a bowl then mash with a fork. Stir in the mayonnaise, harissa paste and lemon juice. Remove the thyme and bay leaves and serve the chicken, potatoes and vegetables with a spoonful of the roasted garlic mayonnaise on the side.

V Try this Quorn fillets make a great vegetarian alternative to chicken. There's no need to brown the Quorn first, simply place 200 g (7 oz) fillets on the potatoes in step 3, spray with the cooking spray and top with the bay leaves. Cook for 20–25 minutes until golden and cooked through.

Did you know?

Browning the chicken before roasting it in the oven not only gives it a lovely golden colour but it also helps to seal in the precious juices and keeps it deliciously moist.

Tortelloni and vegetables en brodo

Calories per serving 257

Takes 30 mins

Serves 2

calorie controlled cooking spray
1 small onion, sliced
1 carrot, peeled and sliced thinly diagonally
3 runner beans, sliced thinly diagonally
600 ml (20 fl oz) vegetable stock
1 courgette, sliced thinly diagonally
110 g (4 oz) spring greens, shredded
225 g (8 oz) fresh tortelloni pasta filled with
    spinach and ricotta
15 g (½ oz) Parmesan cheese shavings
2 teaspoons low fat pesto
salt and freshly ground black pepper
a few fresh basil leaves, to garnish

This stuffed pasta soup makes a light and summery supper dish or lunch.

1   Heat a large, lidded, non stick saucepan. Spray with the cooking spray and cook the onion, covered, for 5 minutes, stirring occasionally. Add the carrot and runner beans and cook for another 2 minutes, stirring regularly.

2   Add the stock, bring to the boil then reduce the heat and simmer for about 6 minutes, partially covered, until the vegetables are almost tender. Add the courgette and spring greens and cook for 2 minutes.

3   Meanwhile, bring a large pan of water to the boil, add the tortelloni and cook according to the packet instructions. Drain and divide between two large shallow bowls.

4   Using a slotted spoon, scoop out the cooked vegetables and divide between the bowls. Pour the stock over and season to taste. Sprinkle with the Parmesan cheese. Top with a spoonful of the pesto and basil leaves.

Chorizo, bean and tomato couscous

Calories per serving 464

Takes 25 mins

stew only

Serves 1

calorie controlled cooking spray
1 small onion, sliced thinly
3 chestnut mushrooms, sliced
30 g (1¼ oz) chorizo sausage, outer layer
    peeled off, diced
1 garlic clove, chopped
2 tomatoes, quartered
75 g (2¾ oz) canned red kidney beans in chilli
    sauce, drained, reserving 3 tablespoons
    of the chilli sauce
a large pinch of dried chilli flakes
50 g (1¾ oz) dried wholewheat couscous
½ a kettleful of boiling water
salt and freshly ground black pepper
2 teaspoons roughly chopped fresh parsley,
    to garnish

Packed with smoky, chilli flavours, this speedy stew for one is delicious.

1   Heat a non stick saucepan and spray with the cooking spray. Cook the onion and mushrooms for 2 minutes, stirring regularly. Add the chorizo and garlic and cook for another 2 minutes until beginning to turn golden.

2   Stir in the tomatoes then the kidney beans, the reserved chilli sauce, chilli flakes and 3 tablespoons of water. Simmer for 5 minutes, stirring to prevent it from sticking to the base of the pan. Season to taste.

3   Meanwhile, put the couscous in a bowl and just cover with boiling water then stir. Cover with a plate and leave to stand for 5 minutes or until the water is absorbed. Season and fluff up the grains with a fork.

4   Spoon the couscous on to a plate and serve with the chorizo stew, sprinkled with parsley.

Honey soy salmon and vegetable stir fry

Calories per serving 309

Takes 25 mins + 30 mins marinating

Serves 4

4 tablespoons light soy sauce
2 teaspoons balsamic vinegar
2 tablespoons clear honey
4 x 125 g (4½ oz) skinless salmon fillets
calorie controlled cooking spray
For the vegetable stir fry
2 large garlic cloves, chopped finely
30 g (1¼ oz) fresh root ginger, grated
350 g (12 oz) pack mixed vegetable stir fry

The marinated salmon has a golden honey glaze and comes with crunchy, stir fried vegetables. Serve with 50 g (1¾ oz) dried brown basmati rice per person, cooked according to the packet instructions.

1 Mix together half of the soy sauce, and all of the balsamic vinegar and honey in a shallow dish. Add the salmon and spoon the marinade over until coated. Cover and leave to marinate for 30 minutes in the fridge.

2 Heat a large non stick frying pan, spray both sides of the salmon with the cooking spray and cook for 3 minutes until golden. Spoon over more marinade, spray with the cooking spray, turn over and cook the salmon for another 3 minutes. Keep warm while stir frying the vegetables.

3 Heat a large wok or non stick frying pan, spray with the cooking spray and stir fry the garlic and ginger for 30 seconds, toss in the vegetables and stir fry for another 3–5 minutes until tender. Add the remaining soy sauce and toss until combined. Serve the salmon on top of the vegetables.

Spaghetti amatriciana

Calories per serving 334

Takes 40 mins

Ⓥ ❄

Serves 1

2 vegetarian bacon rashers, chopped roughly
calorie controlled cooking spray
½ onion, chopped
1 large garlic clove, chopped
125 g (4½ oz) passata
1 teaspoon tomato ketchup
a large pinch of dried chilli flakes (optional)
30 g (1¼ oz) frozen petit pois
60 g (2 oz) dried wholemeal spaghetti
salt and freshly ground black pepper

This vegetarian version of the classic Italian pasta dish features meat-free bacon rashers in a tomato and pea sauce. Serve with broccoli florets.

1 Heat a lidded non stick saucepan. Spray the bacon with the cooking spray, and cook for 3–4 minutes until starting to colour.

2 Add the onion to the pan, spray again with cooking spray and cook, covered and stirring occasionally, for 8 minutes until softened. Add the garlic and cook for another minute.

3 Add the passata and ketchup to the pan, bring to the boil, reduce the heat to low and simmer, partially covered, for 8–10 minutes until reduced and thickened. Stir in the chilli flakes, if using, and peas and cook for a minute or so until tender.

4 Meanwhile, bring a large pan of water to the boil, add the pasta, and cook according to the packet instructions. Drain, reserving 2 tablespoons of the cooking water.

5 Stir the pasta, reserved cooking water and bacon into the tomato sauce and turn until coated. Season then serve immediately.

Crispy potato and meatball pan fry

Calories per serving 313

Takes 40 mins

Serves 4

400 g (14 oz) potatoes, peeled and halved, if large
400 g (14 oz) lean beef mince
1 teaspoon dried thyme
calorie controlled cooking spray
1 leek, sliced thickly
1 courgette, sliced thickly
1 teaspoon cornflour
3 tablespoons red onion chutney
250 ml (9 fl oz) vegetable stock
3 long fresh rosemary sprigs
200 g (7 oz) cherry tomatoes, halved
75 g (2¾ oz) mozzarella light, torn into pieces
salt and freshly ground black pepper

This simple meal is a perfect weekday supper served with 50 g (1¾ oz) shredded Savoy cabbage and 50 g (1¾ oz) peas per person.

1 Bring a saucepan of water to the boil, add the potatoes and cook until tender, then drain and leave to cool slightly. Slice the potatoes thickly and set aside. Meanwhile, mix the mince and thyme together, season and form into 16 walnut sized balls.

2 Heat a large, deep-sided, ovenproof, non stick frying pan. Spray with the cooking spray, add the meatballs and fry over a medium heat for 8 minutes, turning occasionally, until browned all over. Remove from the heat and set aside.

3 Preheat the grill to high. Meanwhile, bring a pan of water to the boil and blanch the leek and courgette for 2 minutes then drain and refresh under cold running water.

4 Stir the cornflour and chutney into the stock and pour into a small pan. Add two sprigs of rosemary then bring to the boil and season with black pepper. Reduce the heat and simmer for 2 minutes until the sauce has reduced and thickened. Remove from the heat and take out the rosemary and discard.

5 Arrange the tomatoes, leek and courgette in the frying pan with the meatballs. Pour the sauce over, then top with the sliced potatoes. Scatter the mozzarella over the top and grill for 6 minutes or until golden.

6 Chop the remaining sprig of rosemary finely and scatter over the top before serving.

(V) Try this For a vegetarian alternative, why not swap the meatballs for 8 x 50 g (1¾ oz) vegetarian Cumberland sausages? Cook for the same length of time as the meatballs in step 2, then slice each one into four and continue the recipe from step 3.

Grow your own...

Why not try to grow your own fresh herbs? It's so convenient to have them to hand and they're very economical too. Thyme and rosemary are good herbs to start with since they're hardy and don't need much looking after.

Picnics & BBQs

Turkey and bacon burgers on page 72

On a warm summer's day, nothing beats a barbecue with good friends and great food. Enjoy delicious dishes for sharing such as the crusty Picnic Loaf, Beef Kebabs in Smoky Barbecue Sauce or Turkey and Bacon Burgers. And, if the sun doesn't shine, you can simply bring the fabulous flavours of summer inside by grilling instead.

Top tips for barbecuing

Barbecued food is fantastic any time of the year but, not only that, many barbecue recipes can also be cooked under the grill, if preferred. To find out how to do this, refer to the individual recipes.

Disposable barbecues

If you're only cooking for two people, a small disposable charcoal barbecue is very convenient to use. Follow the instructions included.

Gas barbecues

~ Gas barbecues use a gas canister as a heat source and it's important that you follow the supplier's safety guidelines before use.

~ Gas is very convenient, less messy and more controllable than charcoal, although you don't get the same smoky flavour.

~ If using a gas barbecue or grill, simply turn it on 5–10 minutes before cooking and follow the recipe.

Charcoal barbecues

Charcoal barbecues require a little more attention than gas ones but the more you use them, the more confident you'll be.

Lighting the barbecue Arrange the charcoal in a heap to one side. It should light easily but use firelighters if you need extra help. As a rough estimate, you should leave the barbecue for around 40 minutes before cooking to allow the flames to die down and the charcoal to turn white. Now spread the charcoal evenly over three-quarters of the base.

If your barbecue is large enough, leave the last quarter of the base as a space to move food to if it's burning or cooking too quickly or to keep food warm.

Cooking To prevent the food from sticking, spray the rack with calorie controlled cooking spray. Place the rack over the heat and now you're ready to barbecue. You can alter the intensity of the heat by varying the height of the racks – obviously the closer to the coals, the hotter it will be.

There are no precise timings for how long to let the barbecue burn before it reaches the correct temperature but, as a rough guide, it should be at its hottest about 40–50 minutes after lighting and it then becomes cooler over time.

You should be able to judge if the barbecue is the right temperature by holding your hand over the heat at a safe distance for a few seconds. With experience, it will become easier to estimate the correct temperature. Be sure to keep an eye on the barbecue and monitor the heat carefully so you can make judgements about the temperature and your cooking. For example, if something is getting too hot and starting to burn, move it to the side.

Kettle barbecues

~ The kettle barbecue is a multi-purpose charcoal barbecue grill with a domed base and lid. When the lid is closed, the heat spreads evenly and circulates freely around the food as it cooks. It's especially good for 'roasting' meats.

~ When lighting a kettle barbecue, the instructions are the same as for the charcoal barbecue, above.

General cooking tips for all barbecues

~ For a successful barbecue, prepare everything in advance. Remove the food from the fridge about 20 minutes before cooking to allow it to come to room temperature.

~ If using wooden skewers, soak them for 30 minutes in advance to prevent them from burning during cooking.

~ Try poaching sausages or ribs in boiling water for a few minutes before cooking, to allow them to cook more evenly and reduce the likelihood of fat dripping.

~ If the meat has been marinated, wipe off any excess to prevent it from dripping through and causing flare ups.

~ It's a good idea to keep a water spray handy to douse any flames, if necessary.

~ Barbecuing is an imprecise method of cooking and times may differ depending on the heat of the barbecue and the varying size and thickness of foods.

~ Searing the outside of red meat, burgers and steaks over a high heat helps to lock in the juices.

~ Sausages and chicken need to be cooked for longer than steaks and require a medium-high heat to prevent the outside from cooking too quickly, burning and leaving the inside under-cooked.

~ Larger pieces of meat, such as ribs, or whole fish need a lower heat, usually medium-high to medium, to allow them to cook evenly and to prevent the outside from charring before the inside is cooked.

Beef takaki on page 82

Tear 'n' share tomato and cheese bread

Calories per serving 53

30 mins prep + 30 mins rising, 35 mins cooking

V ❄ **Makes 14 rolls as one loaf**

40 g (1½ oz) sun-dried tomatoes
½ a kettleful of boiling water
calorie controlled cooking spray
2 tablespoons plain flour, for dusting
500 g (1 lb 2 oz) packet white bread mix
2 garlic cloves, sliced thinly
1 teaspoon dried oregano
30 g (1¼ oz) half fat mature Cheddar cheese,
    grated

This loaf makes use of a ready prepared bread mix and it's then studded with slivers of garlic and sun-dried tomato and topped with cheese.

1 Soak the sun-dried tomatoes in the boiling water for 20 minutes. Spray a non stick baking sheet with the cooking spray then dust with flour.

2 Prepare the bread following the packet instructions then after the final rise, divide into fourteen pieces and roll into balls.

3 Drain the tomatoes, and using your hands, squeeze out any excess water then chop into small pieces.

4 Preheat the oven to Gas Mark 7/220°C/fan oven 200°C. Flatten each ball slightly and divide the tomatoes and garlic between the 14 balls of dough. Place in the middle, and bring up the sides of the dough to encase the filling.

5 On the baking sheet, press the balls together two by two to make a long loaf with one roll placed at each end to form a 'point'. Sprinkle the oregano over the top, followed by the cheese. Bake for 30–35 minutes until golden. Leave to cool on a wire rack then separate into fourteen pieces.

Turkey and apple salad

Calories per serving 162

Takes 20 mins

Serves 4

1 green apple, unpeeled, halved, cored, then
    sliced thinly
4 teaspoons lemon juice
1 pitta bread, split open
calorie controlled cooking spray
4 tablespoons low fat natural yogurt
2 tablespoons extra light mayonnaise
1 teaspoon wholegrain mustard
1 small garlic clove, crushed
140 g (5 oz) red cabbage, shredded finely
1 large carrot, peeled and grated finely
200 g (7 oz) cooked skinless turkey breast, cut into
    bite size pieces
salt and freshly ground black pepper
leaves from 2 fresh mint sprigs, to garnish

If you're taking this to a picnic, it's best to add the toasted pitta bread just before serving to prevent it from turning soggy.

1 Preheat the grill to high. Toss the sliced apple in 1 teaspoon of the lemon juice to prevent it from browning. Spray both sides of the pitta with the cooking spray and toast under the grill for a few minutes until golden and crisp. Remove from the heat and leave to cool.

2 Meanwhile, make the dressing. Mix together the yogurt, mayonnaise, remaining lemon juice, mustard and garlic, and season.

3 Arrange the cabbage on a serving plate and top with the carrot, apple and turkey. Drizzle over the dressing. Break the pitta into large, bite size pieces and scatter over the salad then sprinkle with the fresh mint.

V **Try this** Try swapping the turkey for 200 g (7 oz) canned chick peas, drained and rinsed, for a delicious vegetarian version.

Picnic loaf

Calories per serving 142

Takes 15 mins

Serves 6

1 x 285 g (10 oz) crusty rustic square loaf
2 tablespoons extra light mayonnaise
2 teaspoons light pesto
60 g (2 oz) canned tuna in spring water, drained
 and flaked
1 tomato, sliced thinly into rounds
3 lettuce leaves
60 g (2 oz) flame roasted red peppers in brine,
 from a jar, drained and sliced
1 celery stick, sliced thinly
6 pitted black olives, sliced
6 large basil leaves
salt and freshly ground black pepper

This version of the French 'pan bagnat', or 'bathed bread', is best prepared a few hours before serving to allow the flavours of the filling to seep into the crusty loaf.

1 Slice the top off the loaf to make a lid then scoop out the inside of the bread, leaving a 1 cm (½ inch) thick shell. Mix together the mayonnaise and pesto, season, then spread all over the inside of the loaf as well as the bottom of the lid, until evenly covered.

2 Spoon the tuna into the bottom of the loaf, top with an even layer of tomato, lettuce, red pepper, celery and olives then top with the basil – the filling should reach the rim of the loaf. Place the lid on top and wrap the loaf in cling film. Weight down with a plate and two cans of food (for example), and chill until ready to serve. To serve, cut into six pieces.

Cook's tips Why not keep the inside of the loaf for another recipe that requires fresh breadcrumbs? You could freeze the breadcrumbs and then use them for the Turkey Balls in Crème Fraîche Sauce on page 50.

Instead of flame roasted red peppers, use raw pepper, de-seeded and sliced into thin strips.

Honey glazed sausages

Calories per serving 220

15 mins prep, 20 mins cooking

Serves 4

8 reduced fat pork sausages
2 tablespoons clear honey
1 tablespoon balsamic vinegar
1 tablespoon dark soy sauce
calorie controlled cooking spray

The whole family will love these golden, sticky sausage skewers. Serve them with the Mango and Herb Couscous (see page 108).

1 Light the barbecue or preheat the oven to Gas Mark 6/200°C/fan oven 180°C. You could also heat the grill to a medium-high heat.

2 Cut each sausage into four pieces. Mix together the honey, balsamic vinegar and soy sauce in a large, shallow dish. Add the sausage pieces and turn until coated.

3 Using eight skewers, thread four pieces of sausage on to a skewer and repeat to make eight skewers in total. Spray the sausages with the cooking spray. Cook on the barbecue at a medium heat, under the grill or in the oven for about 15–20 minutes, turning occasionally, until cooked through and golden.

4 Remove the sausages from the heat and serve two skewers per person.

Giant 'sausage' roll

Calories per serving 125

15 mins prep, 45 mins cooking

❄

Serves 6

calorie controlled cooking spray
285 g (10 oz) extra lean pork mince (5% fat or less)
2 garlic cloves, chopped finely
30 g (1¼ oz) fresh breadcrumbs
1 apple, unpeeled, cored and grated
2 tablespoons chopped fresh sage
2 teaspoons wholegrain mustard
2 x 45 g (1½ oz) sheets filo pastry, measuring
    50 x 24 cm (20 x 9½ inches), defrosted if frozen
1 tablespoon skimmed milk, for brushing
salt and freshly ground black pepper

If you want to take this on a picnic, wrap it up whole in foil and then slice just before serving.

1 Preheat the oven to Gas Mark 6/200°C/fan oven 180°C. Spray a non stick baking tray with the cooking spray.

2 Put the pork mince in a bowl with the garlic, breadcrumbs, apple, sage and mustard and season well. Stir until combined.

3 Lay out a sheet of the filo, spray with the cooking spray and then top with a second sheet of filo then fold them in half crossways. Spoon the pork mixture down the centre of the filo in a sausage shape. Fold the filo over the filling and wet the edges with a drop of water on your fingers to seal then tuck in the ends to make a large sausage roll shape.

4 Place the filo roll on the baking tray and brush with the milk. Bake for 40–45 minutes until golden and cooked through.

Turkey and bacon burgers

Calories per serving 203

10 mins prep + 30 mins chilling, 15 mins cooking

Serves 4

75 g (2¾ oz) lean back bacon, rind removed,
    chopped into small pieces
400 g (14 oz) turkey mince
1 egg, beaten lightly
2 spring onions, chopped finely
calorie controlled cooking spray
salt and freshly ground black pepper
For the tomato relish
3 tomatoes, halved, de-seeded and diced
½ red onion, chopped finely
1 tablespoon chopped flat leaf parsley
1 tablespoon lime juice

These succulent burgers come with a tomato relish and can be served in a 40 g (1½ oz) crusty roll with Sweetcorn in Sweet Chilli Sauce (see page 114).

1 Light the barbecue or heat the grill in step 3. Put the bacon, turkey, egg, spring onions and seasoning in a large bowl and mix together until thoroughly combined.

2 Form the mixture into four burgers (it is quite soft but will hold together when cooked). Put them on a plate, cover with cling film and chill for 30 minutes.

3 If using a grill, heat it to medium-high now. Meanwhile, prepare the tomato relish. Put the tomatoes, red onion, parsley and lime juice in a small bowl then season. Set aside.

4 Spray each burger with the cooking spray. Cook over a medium-high heat on the barbecue or under the grill for 6 minutes on each side or until cooked and golden and there is no trace of pink inside. Serve the burgers topped with a generous spoonful of relish.

Try this You could use the same weight of chicken mince instead of turkey.

Watermelon, feta and mint salad

Calories per serving 144

Takes 10 mins

(V) Serves 2

¼ small watermelon
75 g (2¾ oz) light feta cheese, cut into bite size cubes
¼ small red onion, sliced thinly
juice of ½ a lime
1 cm (½ inch) strip lime zest, cut into fine shreds
10 fresh mint leaves
freshly ground black pepper

This vibrant salad makes a refreshing addition to a picnic or barbecue and would also work well as a packed lunch.

1 Slice the watermelon away from the rind and remove any seeds, then cut the fruit into 1 cm (½ inch) cubes so you have about 250 g (9 oz) fruit.

2 Put the watermelon in a bowl with the feta and red onion.

3 Squeeze the lime juice over the salad then scatter over the lime zest and mint leaves. Season with black pepper.

Layered omelette pie

Calories per serving 217

Takes 30 mins

Serves 6

calorie controlled cooking spray
9 eggs
60 g (2 oz) thickly cut lean smoked ham, trimmed of visible fat and diced
150 g (5½ oz) light mozzarella cheese, sliced
75 g (2¾ oz) frozen petit pois
2 spring onions, sliced thinly
2 tomatoes, de-seeded and diced
salt and freshly ground black pepper
a handful of fresh basil leaves, to decorate

1 Preheat the oven to Gas Mark 6/200°C/fan oven 180°C. Spray a non stick baking sheet with the cooking spray.

2 Lightly beat together three of the eggs and season. Heat an 18 cm (7 inch) heavy based, lidded, non stick frying pan and spray with the cooking spray. Pour in the eggs and cook, pulling the runny egg into the middle of the pan using a spatula, until the eggs start to set. When nearly set, smooth the top of the omelette and scatter over the ham. Shake to loosen the omelette and slip it on to the baking sheet. Sprinkle the top with half the mozzarella then place in the oven.

3 Wipe the frying pan and spray with the cooking spray, add the peas and spring onions and cook for about 3 minutes until softened. Beat three more of the eggs, season, and pour them into the pan with the peas and onions. Follow the instructions for cooking the first omelette. Remove the first omelette from the oven and carefully slip the second one on top then scatter over the remaining mozzarella. Return it to the oven.

4 Wipe the frying pan and spray again with the cooking spray. Lightly beat the three remaining eggs, season and pour into the pan. Follow the instructions for cooking the first omelette. Just before the omelette is set, scatter over the tomatoes, cover with a lid, and cook for another 2 minutes.

5 Remove the omelettes from the oven and carefully place the third one on top. Leave to cool slightly then scatter over the fresh basil before cutting into six wedges.

(V) **Try this** For a vegetarian version, swap the smoked ham for 60 g (2 oz) Quorn slices.

Beef kebabs in smoky barbecue sauce

Calories per serving 193

Takes 30 mins + 1 hr marinating

Serves 4

375 g (13 oz) lean beef fillet steak, visible fat
    removed, cut into 24 large bite size cubes
1 large red onion, peeled and cut into 16 wedges
16 cherry tomatoes
calorie controlled cooking spray

For the marinade
4 tablespoons tomato paste
4 teaspoons Worcestershire sauce
1 heaped teaspoon smoked paprika
3 teaspoons cider vinegar

To serve
1 small cucumber, sliced into ribbons
8 radishes, sliced thinly into rounds
1 tablespoon lime juice, plus wedges to serve
1 tablespoon chopped fresh mint
salt

The marinade for these beef kebabs is wonderfully rich and intense and would also work well with chicken or pork. Serve with the BBQ Sweet Potato Chips (see page 114).

1 Mix together the ingredients for the marinade in a large, shallow dish. Add the beef, turn until coated then leave to marinate for at least 1 hour or preferably overnight.

2 Light the barbecue or heat the grill to medium-high. You will need eight skewers. On one skewer, thread on a wedge of onion, followed by a piece of beef, a tomato, more beef, onion, tomato, and finally a piece of beef to secure. Repeat to make eight skewers in total.

3 Spoon some of the marinade over the skewers then spray with the cooking spray. Barbecue over a medium-high heat or cook under the grill for 2–3 minutes on each side, basting with more of the marinade to prevent the beef from drying out.

4 Divide the cucumber and radishes between four plates. Pour over the lime juice, season with salt and sprinkle with the mint. Serve two skewers per person, accompanied by lime wedges.

Try this Instead of the beef, try large cubes of tofu instead. Marinate 300 g (10½ oz) firm tofu (pat dry first to remove any liquid) then thread on to skewers with the vegetables and barbecue for 12–15 minutes, turning occasionally.

Marinate…

Marinating is one of the best and easiest ways to add flavour to meat, seafood and vegetables. The longer you leave an ingredient to marinate, the more intensely flavoured the end result will be.

Harissa lamb with courgette tzatziki

Calories per serving 257

Takes 25 mins + 1 hr marinating

Serves 4

2 teaspoons harissa paste

1 tablespoon lime juice

2 x 200 g (7 oz) lean lamb steaks, trimmed of visible fat

calorie controlled cooking spray

4 x 50 g (1¾ oz) Mediterranean flatbreads

3 tablespoons chopped fresh mint

3 tablespoons chopped fresh coriander

1 tablespoon snipped fresh chives

4 tomatoes, de-seeded and diced

salt and freshly ground black pepper

For the courgette tzatziki

5 tablespoons 0% fat Greek yogurt

2 tablespoons lemon juice

1 small garlic clove, crushed

½ courgette, grated coarsely

Lamb is the perfect meat for the barbecue and goes so well with these interesting flavours.

1 Mix together the harissa paste and lime juice in a shallow dish, season then add the lamb and spoon over the marinade, turning the lamb until coated. Leave to marinate, covered, in the fridge for at least 1 hour or preferably overnight.

2 Light the barbecue or heat a non stick frying pan over a medium-high heat. Mix together the ingredients for the tzatziki with 1 tablespoon of water and season.

3 Remove the lamb from the marinade, spray with the cooking spray and cook for 4 minutes on each side or until cooked to your liking. Remove from the heat and leave to rest, covered, for 5 minutes.

4 Wrap the flatbreads in foil and warm on the barbecue or under the grill for a few minutes. Divide the flatbreads between four plates. Cut the lamb into 1 cm (½ inch) diagonal slices and place on the bread. Scatter over the herbs and tomatoes then top each serving with 2 tablespoons of the tzatziki. Serve flat or folded in half, as preferred.

Falafel burgers

Calories per serving 187

Takes 30 mins + 30 mins chilling

V ☼ cooked burgers only   **Serves 4**

400 g can chick peas, drained and rinsed

60 g (2 oz) fresh breadcrumbs

1 tablespoon onion chutney

4 spring onions, sliced thinly

1 large garlic clove, crushed

1 teaspoon ground cumin

1 teaspoon ground coriander

3 tablespoons chopped fresh coriander

1 egg

2 tablespoons plain flour, for dusting

2 tablespoons reduced fat houmous

2 tablespoons 0% fat Greek yogurt

2 teaspoons lemon juice

½ teaspoon harissa paste (optional)

calorie controlled cooking spray

salt and freshly ground black pepper

1 Place the chick peas in a food processor and coarsely blend, then add the breadcrumbs, chutney, spring onions, garlic, spices, fresh coriander and egg. Season then whizz until mixed to a coarse paste.

2 Dust your hands and work surface with the flour and form the mixture into four burgers, about 1 cm (½ inch) thick. (The mixture is quite loose but the burgers hold together after chilling.) Put the burgers on a plate, uncovered, and refrigerate for 30 minutes.

3 Light the barbecue or heat the grill to medium-high. Meanwhile, make the sauce. Mix together the houmous, yogurt, lemon juice and harissa paste, if using, in a bowl.

4 Spray the burgers with the cooking spray and barbecue or grill over a medium heat for 5 minutes each side until golden. Serve the burgers with a spoonful of the sauce by the side.

Cook's tip Top these chick pea burgers with a spoonful of homemade gazpacho salsa: mix together diced tomatoes and chopped red onion, cucumber, mint and red chilli then finish with a squeeze of lime juice.

Barbecued vegetable platter

Calories per serving 136

20 mins prep + 1 hr marinating, 25 mins cooking

(V)   **Serves 4**

275 g (9½ oz) butternut squash, peeled,
    de-seeded and cut into 1 cm (½ inch)
    thick half-moon shaped slices
12 asparagus spears, wooden stalks trimmed
2 courgettes, sliced lengthways
12 mushrooms, trimmed
1 large red onion, halved with stem intact, and cut
    into 8 wedges
1 small aubergine, sliced into 1 cm (½ inch)
    rounds then halved
1 large yellow pepper, de-seeded and cut into
    8 wedges
calorie controlled cooking spray
salt and freshly ground black pepper
For the marinade
3 tablespoons dark soy sauce
1 tablespoon balsamic vinegar
1 teaspoon olive oil
1 teaspoon dried or 1 tablespoon chopped
    fresh oregano
1 teaspoon dried or 1 tablespoon chopped
    fresh thyme

Vegetables take on a delicious caramelised sweetness when barbecued. This colourful selection of marinated fresh vegetables can be served with a creamy avocado dip, as described below.

1 To make the marinade mix together all the ingredients in a large, shallow dish. Add the vegetables, season and turn with your hands until they are coated in the marinade. Cover and leave to marinate for about 1 hour.

2 Meanwhile, light the barbecue or heat the grill to medium-high. Using tongs, remove the vegetables from the dish on to a plate, reserving the marinade, and spray them with the cooking spray. Start cooking the squash first and barbecue or grill for 25 minutes, turning halfway, or until golden and tender.

3 After 10 minutes, arrange the pepper, mushrooms, onion wedges and aubergine on the rack and barbecue or grill for 15 minutes, turning halfway, or until tender and charred in places.

4 After 5 minutes, arrange the asparagus and courgette on the rack and barbecue or grill for 10 minutes, turning halfway, or until tender and charred in places.

5 Place all the cooked vegetables on a serving platter and spoon over some of the marinade before serving.

Cook's tip If grilling, you'll need to cook the vegetables in batches so, as you go, place the cooked vegetables on the serving platter.

Dip in...

To make an avocado dip, put the flesh from 1 small, ripe avocado (about 150 g/5½ oz) with the juice and finely grated zest of a lime, 5 tablespoons of virtually fat free fromage frais and ½ a teaspoon of dried chilli flakes in a blender and whizz until smooth and creamy. Season with salt to taste. Alternatively, mash with a fork. Serve 1 tablespoon per person.

Pan Catalan

Calories per serving 145

Takes 20 mins

Serves 4

200 g (7 oz) day old crusty loaf, such as ciabatta,
    halved lengthways
calorie controlled cooking spray
1 large garlic clove, halved
2 tomatoes, halved
40 g (1½ oz) Serrano ham (about 4 slices),
    trimmed of fat
salt and freshly ground black pepper
a handful of fresh basil leaves, to garnish

Bread takes on a new dimension when barbecued, acquiring a slightly smoky flavour, so it's well worth trying it.

1 Light the barbecue or heat a griddle pan over a medium-high heat. Slice each bread half in two to make four pieces in total.

2 Spray the uncut side of the bread with the cooking spray and cook for about 3 minutes, pressing down the bread to flatten it. Spray the cut side with the cooking spray and place cut side down on the barbecue or griddle pan for another 3 minutes, or until toasted and charred in places.

3 Remove the bread from the heat and rub the top with the cut side of the garlic. Squeeze the juice from one tomato over each slice of bread, rubbing it in, then dice the remaining pulp and skin and season.

4 Arrange a slice of ham on top of the bread and scatter over the diced tomato. Garnish with a few basil leaves before serving.

Beef tataki

Calories per serving 264

Takes 30 mins

Serves 2

100 g (3½ oz) Little Gem lettuce, shredded
30 g (1¼ oz) pea shoots
½ small red onion, sliced thinly into rings
2.5 cm (1 inch) cucumber, quartered,
    de-seeded and sliced thinly
4 radishes, sliced thinly into rounds
2 x 150 g (5½ oz) lean beef fillet steaks
calorie controlled cooking spray
For the dressing
1 tablespoon light soy sauce
1 tablespoon lime juice
½ teaspoon caster sugar
1 teaspoon grated fresh root ginger
salt and freshly ground black pepper

In Japanese, the word 'tataki' means 'to sear on the outside'. In this recipe, the steaks are seared on the barbecue then served with an exotic salad.

1 Light the barbecue or preheat the grill to high. Mix together the ingredients for the dressing and season with black pepper. Arrange the lettuce and pea shoots on a serving plate then top with the red onion, cucumber and radishes.

2 Spray the steak with the cooking spray and season. Barbecue over a high heat or cook under the grill for about 1–2 minutes on each side or until cooked to your liking. Remove from the heat then leave to rest, covered, for 5 minutes.

3 Slice each steak across the grain then arrange on top of the salad. Drizzle the dressing over the top.

Sticky duck with nectarines

Calories per serving 252

20 mins prep + 1 hr marinating, 15 mins cooking

Serves 2

2 x 125 g (4½ oz) skinless duck breasts
calorie controlled cooking spray
2 just ripe nectarines, halved and stoned
1 teaspoon clear honey

For the marinade
1 tablespoon plum sauce or honey
2 tablespoons light soy sauce
½ teaspoon ground allspice
1 tablespoon grated fresh root ginger
salt and freshly ground black pepper

The Minted Soya Beans and Leeks (see page 106) are perfect with this dish.

1 Mix together all the ingredients for the marinade in a shallow dish, season and add the duck breasts. Spoon the marinade over the duck and leave to marinate, covered, in the fridge for at least 1 hour.

2 Light the barbecue or heat the grill to a medium-high heat. Spray the duck with the cooking spray then cook for 10 minutes, turning once and spooning over more marinade. Remove the duck from the heat and leave to rest for 10 minutes, cover and keep warm.

3 While the duck is resting, spray the cut side of each nectarine with cooking spray and brush with the honey then cook, cut side down for 3–5 minutes, turning once, until golden.

(V) Try this Try swapping the duck with 110 g (4 oz) Quorn fillets (about two) per person. Prepare and cook them in the same way as the duck.

Chicken with lemon, bay and rosemary

Calories per serving 219

15 mins prep, 20 mins cooking

Serves 2

2 x 175 g (6 oz) skinless boneless chicken breasts
2 garlic cloves, sliced thinly
2 large bay leaves
4 lemon slices
2 long and woody fresh rosemary stalks
calorie controlled cooking spray
salt and freshly ground black pepper

Serve with the BBQ Sweet Potato Chips (see page 114) and the Tomato, Red Onion and Mint Salad (see page 108).

1 Light the barbecue or heat the grill to medium-high heat. Make a slit along the side of each chicken breast and open out slightly to make a pocket. Bash the chicken with a meat mallet or the end of a rolling pin to flatten it slightly.

2 Fill the pockets with the sliced garlic, bay leaves and lemon slices. Secure the lemon inside the chicken with the rosemary stalks or some skewers. Spray each side with the cooking spray and season.

3 Cook the chicken for about 8–10 minutes on each side, pressing down occasionally with a spatula, until charred in places and there is no trace of pink inside. Serve immediately.

Lime and coriander salmon skewers

Calories per serving 295

Takes 20 mins + 30 mins marinating

Serves 4

4 x 140 g (5 oz) salmon fillets, skinned
4 tablespoons soy sauce
½ teaspoon caster sugar
4 tablespoons lime juice
¼ teaspoon dried chilli flakes
2 tablespoons chopped fresh coriander
calorie controlled cooking spray
salt and freshly ground black pepper
For the cucumber raita
5 cm (2 inch) cucumber, halved lengthways
6 tablespoons very low fat fromage frais

Firm fish, such as salmon, works well on a barbecue since it keeps its shape during cooking. These slightly spicy skewers are served with a cooling cucumber raita. You could also serve them with BBQ Sweet Potato Chips (see page 114).

1 Cut each salmon fillet into six 2.5 cm (1 inch) cubes. Mix together the soy sauce, caster sugar, 2 tablespoons of lime juice, chilli flakes and half of the coriander in a shallow dish. Season and add the fish. Turn to coat in the marinade and marinate, covered, in the fridge for 30 minutes.

2 Light the barbecue or heat the grill to a medium-high heat. Meanwhile, using a teaspoon scoop out and discard the seeds from the cucumber then grate coarsely. Put the cucumber in a small bowl and combine with the fromage frais and remaining lime juice and coriander. Season and set aside until ready to serve.

3 Thread three cubes of salmon on to a skewer then repeat to make eight skewers in total. Spoon over the marinade, spray with the cooking spray and barbecue over a medium heat or cook under the grill for about 6 minutes, turning the skewers occasionally, until golden and cooked.

4 Serve two skewers per person with a spoonful of the cucumber raita.

Tasty twist...

Ketjap manis is a sweet Indonesian soy sauce and could be used instead of the soy sauce and caster sugar in the marinade. It's available in the oriental section of major supermarkets or Asian food stores.

Honey and ginger scallops

Calories per serving 134

Takes 20 mins + 1 hr marinating

Serves 2

2 tablespoons orange juice
1 tablespoon light soy sauce
1 tablespoon honey
1 teaspoon finely chopped fresh root ginger
1 tablespoon rice vinegar
8 scallops, without the coral
calorie controlled cooking spray
½ medium size red chilli, de-seeded and
    chopped finely
1 tablespoon chopped fresh coriander
salt and freshly ground black pepper
2 thin lime wedges, to serve
For the pea and mint purée
110 g (4 oz) frozen petit pois
2 tablespoons skimmed milk
1 teaspoon half fat crème fraîche
1 tablespoon chopped fresh mint

Succulent and sweet, scallops only take a matter of minutes to cook and make a special treat.

1   Mix together the orange juice, soy sauce, honey, ginger and rice vinegar in a large, shallow dish. Season then add the scallops and turn to coat them in the marinade. Cover and marinate in the fridge for up to 1 hour (but no longer or the scallops will start to 'cook' in the orange juice).

2   To make the pea and mint purée, bring a saucepan of water to the boil, add the petit pois and cook for 2–3 minutes or until tender. Drain then return to the pan with the milk and crème fraîche. Warm through, then mash the peas with a potato masher or fork to a coarse purée. Stir in the mint then season to taste.

3   Light the barbecue or heat a non stick frying pan to a high heat and spray with cooking spray. Remove the scallops from the marinade and spray them with the cooking spray. Thread two scallops on to each of two skewers and cook on the barbecue, or pan fry, for 1 minute on each side, until seared and golden. Scatter the chilli and coriander over the scallops and serve two skewers per person with wedges of lime and the minty pea purée.

Try this You could also try serving squid in the same way. Slice down the sides of 285 g (10 oz) prepared and cleaned squid. Cut each squid into two halves and score the outside in a diamond pattern. Marinate as above then barbecue or pan fry for 1 minute on each side until seared and golden.

Fresh fish...

In the supermarkets, you can buy prepared fresh scallops in packs but you may also like to buy them fresh from the fishmonger who will prepare them for you if you ask.

Cooking for friends

Roast pork with apricot stuffing on page 100

When friends come round, it's time to relax together and enjoy some fabulous food. For the ideal Sunday lunch, serve the Roast Pork with Apricot Stuffing. And when you want to treat everyone to something special, try the Smoked Salmon Sushi as an elegant starter followed by the incredibly delicious Roasted Lemongrass Chicken.

Venison steaks with berry sauce

Calories per serving 235

Takes 20 mins + 30 mins marinating

Serves 4

2 tablepoons soy sauce

2 teaspoons clear honey

4 x 140 g (5 oz) venison loin steaks, trimmed of
   visible fat and cut into bite size pieces

calorie controlled cooking spray

salt and freshly ground black pepper

For the berry sauce

125 ml (4 fl oz) fresh orange juice

2 tablespoons soft brown sugar

2 star anise

1 teaspoon ground allspice

250 g (9 oz) frozen mixed fruit of the forest

zest of 1 orange

Serve with 100 g (3½ oz) new potatoes per person and green beans.

1 Mix together the soy sauce, honey and seasoning. Add the venison and turn to coat in the marinade. Leave to marinate for 30 minutes in the fridge, occasionally spooning the marinade over the meat.

2 Make the berry sauce. Put the orange juice, sugar, star anise and allspice in a pan, bring to the boil then reduce the heat and stir over a gentle heat until the sugar dissolves. Add the berries and orange zest and cook gently for 5 minutes until softened and the sauce has reduced.

3 Heat a non stick frying pan until almost smoking. Remove the venison from the marinade, spray with the cooking spray and cook for 2–3 minutes on each side or until cooked to your liking. Serve the steaks accompanied by the berry sauce.

Spicy beef chilli

Calories per serving 183

25 mins prep, 45 mins cooking

Serves 6

400 g (14 oz) lean stewing beef, trimmed of visible
   fat and cut into small pieces

calorie controlled cooking spray

1 onion, sliced

3 garlic cloves, chopped

350 g (12 oz) butternut squash, peeled,
   de-seeded and cut into 1 cm (½ inch) cubes

400 g can chopped tomatoes

1 tablespoon tomato paste

½ teaspoon ground cinnamon

¼–½ teaspoon dried chilli flakes

2 flame roasted peppers from a jar, about 150 g
   (5½ oz), drained and chopped

10 g (¼ oz) plain chocolate

400 g can black eyed beans, drained and rinsed

3 tablespoons chopped fresh coriander

salt and freshly ground black pepper

Serve with a 200 g (7 oz) jacket potato per person, baked in its skin.

1 Heat a large lidded casserole dish. Spray the beef with the cooking spray and season. Cook the meat in batches for about 3 minutes until browned all over. Remove from the pan and cover.

2 Add the onion to the casserole dish, spray with the cooking spray and cook, covered, for 5 minutes until softened. Add the garlic and squash, then cook for a further 5 minutes.

3 Return the beef to the casserole dish with the chopped tomatoes, 150 ml (5 fl oz) water, tomato paste and spices then bring to the boil. Reduce the heat and simmer, partially covered, for 30 minutes. Add the peppers and chocolate then stir until the chocolate has melted.

4 Add the beans and half of the coriander. Season and simmer for another 10–15 minutes, half-covered. Serve sprinkled with the remaining coriander.

V **Try this** Replace the beef with the same weight of Quorn pieces. Add with the beans in step 4.

Piri piri chicken

Calories per serving 221

15 mins prep + 1 hr marinating, 20 mins cooking

Serves 4

1 large red pepper, de-seeded and sliced
1 large garlic clove, halved
1 teaspoon paprika
2 tablespoons red wine vinegar
4 x 165 g (5¾ oz) skinless boneless chicken breasts
calorie controlled cooking spray
salt and freshly ground black pepper

Serve with 40 g (1½ oz) dried wholewheat couscous per person, cooked according to the packet instructions, and some salad leaves dressed in lemon juice.

1 Put the pepper, garlic, paprika, vinegar and seasoning in a food processor, or use a hand blender, and whizz to a coarse paste.

2 Make three slashes diagonally across each chicken breast. Place in a non metallic roasting dish, spoon over the marinade and marinate in the fridge for at least 1 hour or overnight, if time allows.

3 Preheat the oven to Gas Mark 6/200°C/fan oven 180°C. Heat a large non stick frying pan, spray the chicken with the cooking spray, and cook for 2 minutes on each side until browned.

4 Put the chicken in the roasting dish, spoon over more of the marinade and roast for 15–20 minutes or until cooked through.

V Try this For a vegetarian alternative, marinate 2 x 55 g (1¾ oz) Quorn fillets per person for 1 hour. Spray with cooking spray and pan fry for about 10 minutes.

Smoked salmon sushi

Calories per serving 60

Takes 40 mins + 1 hr chilling

Makes 20 squares

200 g (7 oz) dried sushi rice
30 ml (1 fl oz) rice wine vinegar
1 teaspoon salt
2 teaspoons caster sugar
200 g (7 oz) sliced smoked salmon
4 teaspoons wasabi paste
1½ sheets nori
4 tablespoons light soy sauce, to serve

1 Put the rice in a bowl, cover with water and leave to sit for 20 minutes then drain and rinse. Transfer the rice to a lidded pan, add 325 ml (11 fl oz) of water and bring to the boil then reduce the heat to low. Cover and cook for about 10 minutes or until the water has been absorbed. Remove from the heat and leave to stand for 10 minutes.

2 Combine the rice wine vinegar, salt and sugar in a small dish. Transfer the rice to a large baking tray, sprinkle over the vinegar mixture and mix gently until the rice is coated. Leave to cool.

3 Line a 23 cm (9 inch) dish with cling film, leaving sufficient excess to fold over the top. Arrange the salmon slices, overlapping each other, in the dish. Place dots of wasabi over the fish then, using a wet knife, spread the rice in an even layer all over the top. Finish with a single layer of nori (you will need to cut them with scissors to fit) then press down.

4 Fold the cling film over to enclose then place a piece of cardboard on top and weigh down. Chill for 1 hour, remove the cardboard and then, using a wet bladed knife, cut into 20 squares. Serve with the soy sauce.

Cook's tip It's important to use sushi rice since it has a soft, sticky texture that makes it stick together well. Look for sushi rice, wasabi and nori sheets in the specialist section in supermarkets or oriental food stores.

Roulade with watercress and cream cheese

Calories per serving 208

25 mins prep, 15 mins cooking

Serves 6

50 g (1¾ oz) low fat spread
50 g (1¾ oz) plain flour
300 ml (10 fl oz) semi skimmed milk
40 g (1½ oz) half fat mature Cheddar cheese, grated
4 eggs, separated
1 tablespoon finely grated Parmesan cheese
salt and freshly ground black pepper

For the filling

75 g (2¾ oz) low fat soft cheese with garlic and herbs
4 tablespoons Quark
1 teaspoon Dijon mustard
60 g (2 oz) watercress, trimmed

This light and cheesy starter is lovely with a simple tomato and basil salad.

1 Preheat the oven to Gas Mark 5/190°C/fan oven 170°C. Line a baking tray with baking parchment.

2 Melt the low fat spread in a non stick saucepan. Add the flour and cook for 1 minute, stirring constantly with a wooden spoon. Gradually stir in the milk. Bring to the boil, stirring, then reduce the heat and cook until the sauce is thick and smooth. Remove from the heat and stir in the Cheddar cheese until melted. Beat in the egg yolks and season.

3 In a clean, grease-free bowl, whisk the egg whites until they form stiff peaks. Fold a spoonful of the egg whites into the cheese sauce then fold in the rest until mixed in, taking care not to lose too much of the air. Pour the mixture on to the lined baking tray and gently spread out into an even layer. Bake for 15 minutes until risen and golden.

4 To make the filling, mix together the soft cheese, Quark and mustard then season. Turn the roulade on to a sheet of baking parchment, sprinkled with the Parmesan and peel off the lining paper. Trim the crisp outer edges.

5 Spread the soft cheese mixture over the roulade. Scatter the watercress down the centre and season. Using the paper as a guide, roll it up from the short end as tightly as possible like a Swiss roll. Cut into six slices to serve.

Pot roast chicken with fennel

Calories per serving 272

20 mins prep, 1¼ hrs cooking

Serves 4

calorie controlled cooking spray
1.5 kg (3 lb 5 oz) chicken
1 fennel bulb, stalks discarded, halved and then cut into 1 cm (½ inch) slices
1 large carrot, peeled and quartered
1 large leek, sliced
1 onion, halved
10 fresh thyme sprigs
2 bay leaves
5 garlic cloves, flattened with the side of a knife
1 teaspoon sugar
200 ml (7 fl oz) dry white wine
salt and freshly ground black pepper

Serve with 100 g (3½ oz) boiled potatoes per person.

1 Preheat the oven to Gas Mark 4/180°C/fan oven 160°C. Spray a heatproof and ovenproof casserole dish with the cooking spray. Season the chicken and place in the dish. Brown over a medium heat, turning it occasionally, until the chicken is browned all over – this will take about 10 minutes and is a bit fiddly.

2 Arrange the fennel, carrot, leek, onion, thyme, bay leaves and garlic around the chicken. Mix the sugar into the wine then pour over the chicken, season, then bring up to the boil. Cover and transfer to the oven.

3 Cook for 45 minutes then remove the lid and cook for another 20–30 minutes until the top of the chicken is browned and cooked.

4 Remove the chicken from the dish and leave to stand for 5 minutes, then carve. Serve 110 g (4 oz) slices of the chicken per person without the skin, with the vegetables and garlic.

Parsi lamb

Calories per serving 195

25 mins prep, 35 mins cooking

Serves 4

5 cloves
2 teaspoons cumin seeds
7 cardamom pods, de-seeded
calorie controlled cooking spray
2 onions, sliced thinly
2 large garlic cloves, chopped finely
40 g (1½ oz) fresh root ginger, grated
375 g (13 oz) lean diced lamb, trimmed of
     visible fat
2 tablespoons tomato paste
½ teaspoon dried chilli flakes
2 tablespoons soft brown sugar
2 tablespoons white wine vinegar
400 g can apricots in natural juice, drained
salt
leaves from 2 fresh mint sprigs, to garnish

Indian parsi cooking involves pairing meat with fruit. In this recipe, lamb and apricots are delicious in a rich cardamom and onion sauce. Serve with 50 g (1¾ oz) dried brown basmati rice per person, cooked according to the packet instructions.

1 Put the cloves, cumin and cardamom seeds in a dry frying pan and heat for about 2 minutes or until the spices smell aromatic and slightly toasted. Toss the pan occasionally to prevent the spices from burning then grind them in a pestle and mortar or grinder. Set aside.

2 Heat a large, lidded, non stick saucepan and spray with the cooking spray. Cook the onions, covered, for 12 minutes, stirring occasionally, until golden and softened. Add a splash of water to the pan if the onions start to stick. Add the garlic, ginger and ground spices and fry for another minute, then remove from the pan.

3 Spray the lamb with the cooking spray, add to the saucepan and cook for about 3 minutes or until browned all over. Return the onions to the pan with 400 ml (14 fl oz) water, tomato paste and chilli flakes.

4 Bring to the boil then cover and reduce the heat to low. Simmer for 30 minutes, stirring occasionally. Partially cover the pan for 20 minutes, then remove the lid for the final 10 minutes until the sauce has reduced.

5 Stir in the sugar and vinegar, cook for 3 minutes then add the apricots, season with salt only, and heat through for a further 2 minutes. Serve sprinkled with the mint leaves.

V **Try this** Why not try swapping the lamb for 400 g (14 oz) vegetarian mince? Add to the pan in step 4 and cook, partially covered, for 10 minutes then remove the lid and cook for another 10 minutes until the sauce has reduced. Continue the recipe from step 5.

Spice it up...

Toasting the spices really brings out their flavours and makes them slightly easier to grind. You could also double the quantity and have some ground spice mix ready for next time. Simply store the spices in an airtight jar in a dark cupboard to keep them fresh.

Roasted lemongrass chicken

Calories per serving 227

20 mins prep + overnight marinating,
1¼ hrs cooking

Serves 4

3 fresh lemongrass stalks, outer layers removed
    and chopped
3 garlic cloves
5 cm (2 inch) piece fresh root ginger, chopped
1 shallot
1 tablespoon caster sugar
½ teaspoon dried chilli flakes
2 tablespoons Thai fish sauce
1 tablespoon light soy sauce
juice and grated zest of 1 lime
1.5 kg (3 lb 5 oz) chicken
salt and freshly ground black pepper

1 Put the lemongrass, garlic, ginger, shallot, sugar, chilli flakes, fish sauce, soy sauce, lime juice and zest in a food processor, or use a hand blender, and whizz to a paste. Season.

2 Gently run your hands under the skin of the chicken to detach it from the carcass. Make 2–3 slashes in each leg.

3 Rub the marinade under the skin and all over the top of the chicken then put it in a plastic bag and seal. Put on a plate and leave to marinate in the fridge for at least 8 hours or overnight.

4 Preheat the oven to Gas Mark 4/180°C/fan oven 160°C. Remove the chicken from the oven, cover with foil and leave to rest. Spoon any marinade left in the bag over the top.

5 Roast for 1¼ hours, occasionally basting with the juices in the tin, or until cooked and there is no trace of pink when the thickest part of the chicken is pierced with a skewer.

6 Cover the chicken with foil and leave to rest for 10 minutes before carving. Serve 110 g (4 oz) chicken without the skin per person.

Roast pork with apricot stuffing

Calories per serving 215

20 mins prep, 15 mins cooking

Serves 4

calorie controlled cooking spray
2 shallots, diced
50 g (1¾ oz) fresh breadcrumbs
1 tablespoon chopped fresh rosemary
1 tablespoon chopped fresh thyme
60 g (2 oz) ready to eat dried apricots, cut into
    small pieces
550 g (1 lb 3 oz) pork tenderloin, trimmed of
    visible fat
salt and freshly ground black pepper

This quick roast pork is delicious with French Petit Pois (see page 118) and roast potatoes.

1 Preheat the oven to Gas Mark 5/190°C/fan oven 170°C. Heat a non stick frying pan, spray with the cooking spray and cook the shallots for 5 minutes until softened. Transfer the shallots to a bowl with the breadcrumbs, rosemary, thyme and apricots. Season and stir until combined.

2 Cut the pork in half crossways then make a cut down the length of each piece of pork to open out the fillet like a book. Flatten the pork using a meat mallet or the end of a rolling pin until about 1 cm (½ inch) thick.

3 Divide the apricot stuffing between the two fillets, spooning it along the centre, then fold over the pork to enclose. Secure with string or with a skewer.

4 Heat a large non stick frying pan, spray the pork with the cooking spray then brown the pork for 2–3 minutes, turning until golden all over. Put the pork in a roasting tin then roast for 12–15 minutes until cooked through. Leave to rest, covered, for 5 minutes then cut into 1 cm (½ inch) thick slices and serve.

Jerusalem artichoke soup

Calories per serving 271

Takes 40 mins

(V) (❄) soup only   **Serves 4**

calorie controlled cooking spray

1 large onion, chopped

1 celery stick, chopped

1 large carrot, peeled and sliced

1 large garlic clove, chopped

500 g (1 lb 2 oz) Jerusalem artichokes, scrubbed or
    peeled and chopped

1.2 litres (2 pints) vegetable stock

150 ml (5 fl oz) skimmed milk

salt and freshly ground black pepper

For the mushroom toasts

200 g (7 oz) chestnut mushrooms, sliced thinly

200 g (7 oz) baguette, cut into 8 slices, crusts
    removed

1 garlic clove, halved

3 fresh thyme sprigs, leaves removed

Jerusalem artichokes have a deliciously nutty flavour and create a wonderful filling soup. Enjoy it with these wonderful mushroom toasts.

1 Heat a large, lidded, non stick saucepan. Spray with the cooking spray and cook the onion, covered, for about 5 minutes until softened. Add the celery, carrot, garlic and artichokes. Cook for a further 5 minutes, stirring occasionally.

2 Pour in the stock and bring to the boil then reduce the heat and simmer for 25 minutes, stirring occasionally, until the vegetables are tender. Using a hand held blender, purée the soup until smooth. Stir the milk into the soup, season, and warm through.

3 Meanwhile, preheat the grill to high. Heat a non stick frying pan, spray with the cooking spray and cook the mushrooms over a medium heat for 5 minutes, stirring regularly. Season. Toast both sides of the baguette slices under the grill then rub one side with the garlic, spoon the mushrooms on top and scatter over a few thyme leaves.

4 Ladle the soup into bowls. Serve with two mushroom toasts per person.

Fish in bacon with puy lentils

Calories per serving 318

Takes 35 mins

                    Serves 4

4 thin slices of lean back bacon, rind removed and
    sliced lengthways in half

4 x 150 g (5½ oz) thick haddock fillets

For the puy lentils

150 g (5½ oz) dried puy lentils

calorie controlled cooking spray

1 large onion, chopped finely

2 large garlic cloves, chopped finely

2 carrots, peeled and diced

2 celery sticks, sliced thinly

200 ml (7 fl oz) vegetable stock

juice of ½ a lemon

1 tablespoon Dijon mustard

2 tablespoons chopped fresh rosemary

1 tablespoon chopped fresh parsley

freshly ground black pepper

1 Preheat the oven to Gas Mark 5/190°C/fan oven 170°C and line a baking tray with baking parchment. In a lidded saucepan, cover the lentils with water and bring to the boil, then reduce the heat and simmer, partially covered, for 25 minutes or until tender. Drain then set aside.

2 Meanwhile, heat a large, lidded, non stick frying pan and spray with the cooking spray. Cook the onion for 5 minutes, stirring occasionally, until softened, adding a splash of water if they start to stick.

3 Add the garlic, carrots and celery to the onion and cook for another 5 minutes, adding a splash of water if the vegetables start to stick. Pour in the stock and lemon juice then simmer, partially covered, for 3 minutes.

4 Wrap two strips of bacon around each haddock fillet, season with black pepper and arrange on a baking tray. Spray each fillet with the cooking spray and roast for 12–15 minutes until cooked.

5 Stir the mustard, herbs and lentils into the vegetables and warm through. Season with black pepper and divide between four plates. Top each serving with a fillet of fish.

Side dishes

Fennel, watercress and clementine salad on page 116

A good side dish can turn a simple meal into something sensational

so get creative and liven up dinnertime with some exciting little twists.

Choose from recipes such as Minted Soya Beans and Leeks, Sesame

Green Beans or Mango and Herb Couscous. And learn the secret to

making Perfectly Cooked Rice every time.

Minted soya beans and leeks

Calories per serving 107

Takes 10 mins

V   **Serves 2**

125 g (4½ oz) soya beans
1 leek, sliced thinly
1 tablespoon lemon juice
2 tablespoons chopped fresh mint
salt and freshly ground black pepper

Firm green soya beans are flavoured with leeks, mint and lemon juice, making them the perfect partner for fish, pork or lamb.

1 Bring about 2.5 cm (1 inch) of water to the boil in a lidded saucepan. Put the soya beans in a steamer basket and place over the boiling water. Cover and steam for 3 minutes then add the leeks and cook for another 2 minutes. Alternatively, bring a saucepan of water to the boil and cook the soya beans and leeks for 2 minutes or until tender, then drain.

2 Tip the soya beans and leeks into a serving bowl. Add the lemon juice and mint then season. Stir gently to combine before serving.

V Try this For an oriental version, you could replace the lemon juice with lime juice and the fresh mint with fresh coriander. Drizzle with 1 tablespoon of light soy sauce.

Cauliflower mash

Calories per serving 34

Takes 15 mins

V ✳   **Serves 4**

calorie controlled cooking spray
1 banana shallot, chopped finely
1 garlic clove, crushed
300 g (10½ oz) cauliflower florets
200 ml (7 fl oz) hot vegetable stock
1 tablespoon half fat crème fraîche

Rediscover the pleasures of cauliflower with this creamy mash. It makes an excellent accompaniment to roasted or grilled meat and fish.

1 Heat a lidded non stick frying pan and spray with the cooking spray. Cook the shallot for 5 minutes, covered, until softened. Add the garlic and cook for another minute.

2 Meanwhile, bring about 2.5 cm (1 inch) water to the boil in a lidded saucepan. Put the cauliflower in a steamer basket and place over the boiling water. Cover and steam for about 4 minutes or until tender. (Alternatively, bring a pan of water to the boil, add the cauliflower and cook for the same length of time until tender, then drain.)

3 Put the shallot and garlic into a blender with the steamed cauliflower, stock and crème fraîche then blend to a smooth purée. (Alternatively, mash with a potato masher.) Reheat gently in a pan and season to taste.

Mango and herb couscous

Calories per serving 189

Takes 15 mins

(V)   **Serves 2**

90 g (3¼ oz) dried wholewheat couscous
½ a kettleful of boiling water
juice of ½ a lemon
1 garlic clove, crushed
1 teaspoon finely chopped fresh root ginger
½ red chilli, de-seeded and chopped finely
2 tablespoons chopped fresh coriander
2 tablespoons chopped fresh mint
2 tablespoons chopped fresh flat leaf parsley
½ ripe mango, peeled, stoned and diced
salt and freshly ground black pepper

The fluffy couscous readily takes on the flavours of the fresh herbs, ginger, chilli and lusciously sweet mango.

1 Put the couscous in a bowl and just cover with boiling water. Stir then cover with a plate. Set aside for 5 minutes until the water is absorbed then fluff up with a fork.

2 Pour the lemon over the couscous and add the garlic, ginger, chilli and herbs. Stir until combined then season to taste. Serve the couscous topped with the fresh mango.

Tomato, red onion and mint salad

Calories per serving 53

Takes 10 mins

(V)   **Serves 1**

2 tomatoes, sliced thinly into rounds
4 radishes, sliced thinly into rounds
2.5 cm (1 inch) cucumber, quartered, de-seeded and sliced thinly
¼ small red onion, sliced thinly into rounds
1 tablespoon lime juice
salt and freshly ground black pepper
1 tablespoon chopped fresh mint, to garnish

A simple, refreshing salad that goes well with lots of different cuisines, ranging from Middle Eastern and Mediterranean to Asian.

1 Arrange the tomatoes and radishes in a shallow serving bowl then scatter over the cucumber and red onion.

2 Drizzle over the lime juice, season to taste and finish with the mint sprinkled over the top.

Cook's tip This salad is best served at room temperature to allow the flavour of the fresh vegetables and mint to marry together.

Slow pan cooked potatoes

Calories per serving 99

15 mins prep, 30 mins cooking

Ⓥ **Serves 4**

15 g (½ oz) low fat spread

425 g (15 oz) potatoes, such as Maris Piper,
peeled and cut thinly into 5 mm (¼ inch) slices

2 garlic cloves, sliced thinly

150 ml (5 fl oz) hot vegetable stock

calorie controlled cooking spray

salt and freshly ground black pepper

Thin slices of potato are cooked slowly over a very low heat until they become meltingly soft and tender.

1 Melt the low fat spread in a large, lidded, non stick frying pan. Spray the potatoes with the cooking spray then arrange half of them in an even layer in the pan. Top with the garlic followed by a second layer of the remaining potatoes.

2 Pour the stock over the top and season. Spray with the cooking spray.

3 Bring to the boiling point then reduce the heat to its lowest setting. Place a circle of baking parchment over the potatoes to fit snugly – this will help to prevent the potatoes from drying out.

4 Cover the pan with a lid and cook, without stirring, for 25–30 minutes or until the potatoes are very tender. The bottom will be golden but try not to let it burn.

Sesame green beans

Calories per serving 36

Takes 15 mins

Ⓥ **Serves 4**

250 g (9 oz) fine green beans, trimmed

1 teaspoon sesame seeds

1 teaspoon sesame oil

1 tablespoon light soy sauce

These beans are equally delicious served warm with oriental dishes or at room temperature as a salad.

1 Bring about 2.5 cm (1 inch) of water to the boil in a lidded saucepan. Put the green beans in a steamer basket and place over the boiling water. Cover and steam for about 4 minutes or until tender. Alternatively, bring a pan of water to the boil, add the beans and cook for 4 minutes or until tender, then drain.

2 Meanwhile, put the sesame seeds in a dry non stick frying pan. Toast for 3–5 minutes until light golden, tossing the pan occasionally. Remove from the pan and set aside.

3 Mix together the sesame oil and light soy sauce then pour over the warm green beans. Scatter over the sesame seeds before serving.

Potato, cucumber and dill salad

Calories per serving 92

Takes 20 mins

(V)   **Serves 4**

400 g (14 oz) baby new potatoes, scrubbed
6 cm (2½ inch) cucumber, quartered, de-seeded
    and sliced thinly
2 spring onions, sliced diagonally
1 tablespoon chopped fresh dill
For the dressing
4 tablespoons fat free fromage frais
1 teaspoon wholegrain mustard
2 teaspoons lemon juice
salt and freshly ground black pepper

This crisp, summery salad goes particularly well with cooked meats, fish and barbecued food.

1 Bring a saucepan of water to the boil, add the potatoes and cook for 10 minutes or until tender then drain. Transfer to a serving bowl and leave to cool slightly. Add the cucumber and spring onions to the bowl.

2 To make the dressing, mix together the fromage frais, mustard and lemon juice. Season and spoon the dressing over the potato salad. Turn until coated. Serve sprinkled with dill.

Perfectly cooked rice

Calories per serving 177

10 mins prep, 25 mins cooking

(V) (❄)   **Serves 4**

200 g (7 oz) dried brown basmati rice

There are many ways to cook rice but this method creates light, fluffy grains and is equally successful with various rice varieties.

1 Rinse the rice in a sieve under cold running water then tip into a medium size, lidded saucepan.

2 Pour in 425 ml (15 fl oz) water. Bring to the boil then reduce the heat to its lowest setting and cover. Simmer for 20–25 minutes, without removing the lid, until the water has been absorbed and the grains are tender.

3 Remove the pan from the heat, and leave to stand, covered, for 5 minutes.

Cook's tip If using white rice, follow the instructions above, reducing the quantity of water to 400 ml (14 fl oz). It will take about 10 minutes to cook until tender. Then cover and leave to stand for 5 minutes.

It's useful to know that 50 g (1¾ oz) dried rice is equivalent to 140 g (5 oz) cooked rice.

(V) **Try this** Flavour the rice with 1 raw green chilli, de-seeded and chopped, 1 tablespoon of toasted coconut, 1 tablespoon of lime juice and the grated zest of 1 lime. It's fantastic with barbecued food.

Sweetcorn in sweet chilli sauce

Calories per serving 51

10 mins prep, 15 mins cooking

Ⓥ   **Serves 4**

2 tablespoons sweet chilli sauce
4 cm (1½ inches) fresh root ginger, grated
juice of ½ a lime
2 corn cobs, halved
salt and freshly ground black pepper

Sweet and succulent, corn-on-the-cob is a barbecue must-have.

1 Light the barbecue and heat until hot or preheat the oven to Gas Mark 6/200°C/fan oven 180°C. Put the chilli sauce in a bowl. Using your hands, squeeze the juice from the ginger into the bowl then stir in the lime juice. Season to taste.

2 Put each corn cob on a piece of foil, large enough to make a parcel. Spoon the chilli sauce mixture over the top, turning until coated. Seal the foil to make a parcel then barbecue over a medium-high heat or cook in the oven for 15 minutes or until tender.

BBQ sweet potato chips

Calories per serving 105

10 mins prep, 15 mins cooking

Ⓥ   **Serves 2**

185 g (6½ oz) sweet potatoes, peeled and sliced
    into rounds, about 5 mm (¼ inch) thick
1 teaspoon olive oil
calorie controlled cooking spray
salt and freshly ground black pepper

Choose the vivid, orange-fleshed sweet potato to make these chips. Not only do they look great, but they also have a slightly sweeter taste.

1 Light the barbecue or preheat the grill to a medium-high heat. Brush the sweet potato with the olive oil and spray with the cooking spray.

2 Barbecue over a medium-high heat for 12–15 minutes or cook under the grill for the same length of time. Turn once, until tender and charred in places. Season to taste.

Ⓥ **Try this** These sweet potato chips are delicious dunked into a garlic mayonnaise. Mix together 3 tablespoons of extra light mayonnaise, 1 small finely chopped garlic clove and 1 tablespoon of skimmed milk. Season to taste then transfer to a serving bowl.

Sweet baby carrots

Calories per serving 78

Takes 15 mins

(V)   **Serves 4**

450 g (1 lb) baby carrots, trimmed
1 tablespoon low fat spread
1 large garlic clove, crushed
2 fresh rosemary sprigs, leaves chopped finely
2 teaspoons wholegrain mustard
1 tablespoon clear honey
calorie controlled cooking spray
salt and freshly ground black pepper

The carrots take on a sticky honey glaze during cooking, which is then made even more delicous by the rosemary and mustard.

1 Bring about 2.5 cm (1 inch) of water to the boil in a lidded saucepan. Put the carrots in a steamer basket and place over the boiling water. Cover and steam for about 3 minutes or until tender. Alternatively, bring a small amount of water to the boil and cook the carrots for 3 minutes or until tender, then drain.

2 Melt the low fat spread in a saucepan, add the garlic and rosemary and sauté for 1 minute.

3 Add the carrots, mustard and honey. Spray with the cooking spray then cook, stirring constantly to prevent the honey from burning, for 2 minutes until the carrots are tender and coated in the sticky glaze. Season to taste and serve.

Fennel, watercress and clementine salad

Calories per serving 53

Takes 5 mins

(V)   **Serves 2**

40 g (1½ oz) watercress, trimmed
60 g (2 oz) fennel, fronds trimmed and sliced thinly
2 clementines, peeled and sliced into rounds
1 teaspoon olive oil
1 teaspoon balsamic vinegar
salt and freshly ground black pepper

Fresh and fragrant, this salad is best made just before serving.

1 Put the watercress in a serving bowl and top with the fennel and then the clementines.

2 Mix together the olive oil and balsamic vinegar, season, then spoon the dressing over the salad just before serving.

Summer vegetables with aioli

Calories per serving 174
Takes 25 mins
(V)   **Serves 2**

175 g (6 oz) broad beans, shelled
8 baby carrots, trimmed
1 small fennel bulb, trimmed and cut into
    8 wedges
12 asparagus spears, trimmed
6 baby courgettes, trimmed and halved
    lengthways
For the aioli
2 tablespoons extra light mayonnaise
2 tablespoons low fat natural yogurt
1 garlic clove, crushed
1 tablespoon lemon juice
salt and freshly ground black pepper

Serve as a light meal with a 40 g (1½ oz) slice of crusty bread and 25 g (1 oz) black olives in brine each.

1 Bring a saucepan of water to the boil, add the broad beans and cook for about 3 minutes or until tender. Drain. Leave for a minute until cool enough to handle then slip the beans out of their grey jackets.

2 Bring about 2.5 cm (1 inch) of water to the boil in a lidded saucepan. Put the carrots and fennel in a steamer basket and place it over the boiling water. Cover and steam for about 3–5 minutes or until tender. Cover with with foil to keep warm and set aside.

3 Bring about 2.5 cm (1 inch) of water to the boil again in the lidded saucepan. Put the asparagus and courgettes in a steamer basket and place it over the boiling water. Steam for about 4 minutes or until tender. Cover the vegetables with foil to keep warm and set aside.

4 Meanwhile, mix together all the ingredients for the aioli in a bowl. Arrange all the vegetables on a serving platter and serve with the aioli dipping sauce on the side.

French petit pois

Calories per serving 44
Takes 10 mins
(V)   **Serves 2**

1 teaspoon low fat spread
1 Little Gem lettuce, shredded
2 spring onions, sliced
60 g (2 oz) frozen petit pois
50 ml (2 fl oz) hot vegetable stock
freshly ground black pepper
a few fresh mint leaves, to garnish (optional)

The delicious combination of peas, Little Gem lettuce and spring onions, poached in a buttery stock goes particularly well with roasts. You could also scatter over a few mint leaves before serving.

1 Melt the spread in a lidded non stick frying pan. Add the lettuce, spring onions, petit pois and stock.

2 Simmer, covered, for 3–5 minutes until the vegetables have softened. Season with black pepper and garnish with a few mint leaves, if using, before serving.

Snacks

Homemade popcorn on page 124

When you fancy a snack, these simple recipes are just what you want.

Not only do they taste wonderful but most are ready in 10 minutes or

less. For a quick and filling fix, make some Mediterranean Toasts or get

popping and treat yourself to Homemade Popcorn with a spicy twist.

Cherry and banana smoothie

Calories per serving 214

Takes 5 mins

(V) (❄)

Serves 1

100 g (3½ oz) frozen cherries, defrosted
1 banana, halved
3 tablespoons low fat plain yogurt
3 tablespoons skimmed milk

Rich and creamy, this smoothie can be whipped up in only 5 minutes.

1 Put the cherries in a blender with the banana, yogurt and milk then blend until smooth and creamy.

2 Pour into a tall glass and serve immediately.

Cook's tips Frozen fruit is often more economical to buy than fresh and it's so convenient to use. Simply defrost the amount you need to avoid any wastage.

The smoothie can be frozen to make a delicious yogurt ice but leave the fruit frozen before blending. Pour into a small freezerproof container and freeze until frozen. Before serving, remove from the freezer for about 20 minutes to soften.

(V) **Try this** Frozen mango, mixed berries or raspberries could all be used instead of the cherries. If using frozen fruit, leave to defrost first and use as instructed above.

Fruit and nut mix

Calories per serving 116

Takes 15 mins

(V)

Serves 4

2 tablespoons sunflower seeds
2 tablespoons pumpkin seeds
2 tablespoons shredded or desiccated
    unsweetened coconut
25 g (1 oz) Special K cereal with berries
15 g (½ oz) ready to eat dried prunes, chopped
    roughly
15 g (½ oz) goji berries

This is the perfect snack when time is short and you're searching for a quick bite to eat. Goji berries are small and red and can be found in the dried fruit section in major supermarkets.

1 Put the sunflower and pumpkin seeds in a dry non stick frying pan and heat gently, stirring occasionally, over a medium-low heat for 3–5 minutes until light golden. Tip into a bowl and leave to cool.

2 Add the coconut to the pan and heat for 2 minutes, stirring regularly, until light golden. Leave to cool.

3 Combine the seeds, coconut, Special K, prunes and goji berries in a bowl. Stir until combined then transfer to an airtight container.

Cook's tip This trail mix can be stored in an airtight container for up to 1 week.

(V) **Try this** The same amount of ready to eat dried apricots can be used instead of prunes.

Honey dried apples

Calories per serving 63

10 mins to prepare, 30 mins to cook

Ⓥ   **Serves 4**

2 apples, unpeeled
2 tablespoons clear honey

These delicious, honey coated slices of dried apple are sure to become one of your favourite snacks.

1 Preheat the oven to Gas Mark 4/180°C/fan oven 160°C. Warm the honey in a small saucepan over a low heat until runny.

2 Using a mandolin or sharp knife, thinly slice the apples into rounds about 3 mm (⅛ inch) thick. Discard any pips (leave the core) then arrange on a wire rack placed over a baking tray. Brush one side with half of the honey.

3 Bake the apples for 15 minutes, turn over and brush the other side with the remaining honey. Bake for another 10–15 minutes or until light golden and crisp.

4 Lay out the apples on a sheet of baking parchment and leave to cool.

Homemade popcorn

Calories per serving 63

Takes 10 mins

Ⓥ   **Serves 4**

60 g (2 oz) popping corn
2 teaspoons Cajun spice mix or Jamaican jerk
    seasoning
grated zest of 1 lemon

This novel way to enjoy shop bought popcorn makes a quick and tasty snack and it's so easy to prepare.

1 Put the popcorn in a lidded microwave container, large enough to allow it to 'pop'. Cover and microwave for 4–6 minutes then transfer to a serving bowl.

2 Add the spices to the bowl and stir until coated. Sprinkle with the lemon zest before serving.

Cook's tip If you don't own a microwave, heat 2 teaspoons of vegetable oil in a medium size lidded saucepan. Add the popping corn, cover, and cook over a medium-low heat until it starts to pop. Shake the pan occasionally, still covered, until all the corn has popped. Transfer to a bowl and flavour as above.

Ⓥ **Try this** For a sweet alternative, follow the microwave instructions. Tip the popcorn into a bowl, pour 3 teaspoons of maple syrup or honey over then stir the popcorn until lightly coated.

Cool dogs

Calories per serving 290

10 mins prep, 15 mins cooking

Serves 2

2 x 50 g (1¾ oz) reduced fat pork sausages
2 low fat tortillas
1 tablespoon extra light mayonnaise
1 tablespoon Dijon mustard
freshly ground black pepper
To serve
4 cocktail gherkins, diced finely
10 cherry tomatoes

This variation on the classic 'hot dog' can be enjoyed warm or cold.

1 Preheat the grill to high and line the grill pan with foil. Grill the sausages, turning occasionally, for 12–15 minutes until cooked through and golden. Allow to cool slightly and then cut the sausages into thin rounds.

2 Warm the tortillas in a dry non stick frying pan for about 3 minutes, turning halfway.

3 Mix together the mayonnaise and mustard and spread over the tortillas. Scatter half of the sausage rounds and half of the gherkins over each. Season with pepper and roll up. Cut in half and serve accompanied by the tomatoes.

V **Try this** You could use vegetarian Quorn sausages instead. Prepare and cook in the same way.

Roast chicken 'roll up'

Calories per serving 147

Takes 5 mins

Serves 1

2 teaspoons low fat soft cheese
1 teaspoon lemon juice
1 small spring onion, chopped finely
2 medium thin slices (75 g/2¾ oz total) of
    roasted chicken
4 long thin strips of red pepper
freshly ground black pepper

A speedy snack for when you're feeling peckish, this chicken 'roll up' would also be ideal for a lunchbox. Serve with sticks of carrot and celery.

1 In a bowl, mix together the soft cheese, lemon juice and spring onion.

2 Spoon the soft cheese mixture down one half of each chicken slice, season with black pepper and then top each with two strips of red pepper.

3 Roll up the chicken slices to encase the filling and wrap in cling film until ready to eat.

Try this Instead of roast chicken, you could use the same weight of roast beef. Stir ½ a teaspoon of horseradish sauce into the soft cheese mixture.

Alternatively, why not try with the same weight of roast pork and replace the red pepper with thin slices of apple?

Rice cakes with toppings

Takes 5 mins   **Serves 1 (per topping)**

Rice cakes make a simple snack and they're the ideal base for all manner of toppings – both sweet and savoury. Look out for a brand that uses wholegrain rice. Here are three suggestions for simple toppings.

Calories per serving 77

40 g (1½ oz) low fat natural cottage cheese
1 wholegrain rice cake
1 ready to eat dried date, cut into small pieces

Cottage cheese and date

1 Spoon the cottage cheese over the rice cake and scatter the chopped date over the top. Serve straightaway.

Calories per serving 115

2 walnut halves
1 tablespoon low fat soft cheese
1 wholegrain rice cake
½ teaspoon clear honey

Soft cheese, honey and walnuts

1 Put the walnut halves in a dry non stick frying pan and toast over a medium-low heat for about 3 minutes, turning once, until lightly browned on both sides. Roughly chop the walnuts into small pieces.
2 Spread the soft cheese over the rice cake, sprinkle with the walnuts then drizzle over the honey before serving.

Calories per serving 64

25 g (1 oz) lean oven roasted ham, trimmed of fat
1 wholegrain rice cake
¼ small pear, about 25 g (1 oz), sliced thinly
    lengthways

Ham and pear

1 Arrange the ham on top of the rice cake then top with the slices of pear.

Raisin and cinnamon soda bread

Calories per serving 108

10 mins prep + 10 mins cooling, 30 mins cooking

V ✱ **Makes 16 wedges**

375 g (13 oz) wholemeal flour, plus
    2 tablespoons for dusting
1 tablespoon caster sugar
1 teaspoon ground cinnamon
1 teaspoon bicarbonate of soda
½–1 teaspoon salt
90 g (3¼ oz) raisins
284 ml carton buttermilk
1 egg, beaten lightly

1 Preheat the oven to Gas Mark 6/200°C/fan oven 180°C. Line a non stick baking sheet with baking parchment.

2 Sift the flour, sugar, cinnamon, bicarbonate of soda and salt into a large mixing bowl. Stir in the raisins until combined then make a well in the centre. Pour in the buttermilk and egg, stir with a fork, then use your fingers to form the mixture into a soft dough.

3 Reserving 1 teaspoon of the flour, spread out the rest on a clean work surface. Tip the dough on to the floured work surface then knead briefly to form a round loaf. Transfer to the prepared baking sheet. Dust the top of the loaf with any reserved flour then make a deep cross into the dough – about three quarters of the way through.

4 Bake for 25–30 minutes until risen and golden. If you tap the bottom of the loaf, it will sound hollow when cooked. Leave to cool on a wire rack for 10 minutes.

V Try this You could add the same amount of goji berries instead of raisins to the loaf.

For a savoury loaf, omit the cinnamon and raisins.

Apricot, oat and hazelnut bars

Calories per serving 96

Takes 20 mins + 1 hr chilling

V **Makes 16**

75 g (2¾ oz) whole rolled porridge oats
50 g (1¾ oz) hazelnuts
2 tablespoons sunflower seeds
2 tablespoons pumpkin seeds
225 g (8 oz) ready to eat dried apricots, cut into
    small pieces
75 g (2¾ oz) raisins
5 tablespoons fresh orange juice

These fruity bars are so easy since you don't need to cook them. They'll keep for up to a week stored in an airtight container.

1 Put the oats in a dry non stick frying pan and toast for 5 minutes, stirring occasionally, over a medium-low heat until beginning to turn golden. Remove from the pan and leave to cool.

2 Put the hazelnuts, sunflower and pumpkin seeds in the pan. Toast, stirring, for 3 minutes until lightly toasted. Leave to cool for 5 minutes.

3 Put the oats, nuts and seeds in a food processor and whizz until chopped finely, then tip into a bowl.

4 Put the apricots, raisins and orange juice in the food processor and whizz to a thick purée. Spoon the fruit into the bowl with the oat mixture. Stir until combined into a thick paste.

5 Line a 25 x 18 cm (10 x 7 inch) baking tin with baking parchment. Tip the fruit mixture into the tin and spread into an even layer about 1 cm (½ inch thick). Chill in the fridge until firm for 1 hour. Cut into 16 pieces.

Cook's tip Whole rolled porridge oats, also called jumbo oats, are milled traditionally and have a thicker, rounder flake than rolled oats.

Homemade oatcakes

Calories per serving 91

20 mins prep + 5 mins cooling, 20 mins cooking

(V)   **Makes 8**

calorie controlled cooking spray
60 g (2 oz) medium oatmeal
75 g (2¾ oz) wholemeal flour, plus 1 tablespoon
    for dusting
¼ teaspoon baking powder
½ teaspoon salt
2 teaspoons caster sugar
50 g (1¾ oz) low fat spread
1–2 tablespoons semi skimmed milk

These oatcakes are delicious with a sweet or savoury topping or they can simply be enjoyed on their own.

1 Preheat the oven to Gas Mark 6/200°C/fan oven 180°C. Spray a non stick baking tray with the cooking spray.

2 Sift the oatmeal, flour, baking powder, salt and caster sugar into a mixing bowl, adding any bran left in the sieve.

3 Using your fingertips, rub in the low fat spread until the mixture resembles breadcrumbs. Pour in the milk and mix with a fork, then mix with your hands to make a firm dough.

4 Turn the dough out on to a lightly dusted work surface then roll out until 5 mm (¼ inch) thick. Using a 6 cm (2½ inch) cutter, cut out eight oatcakes, re-rolling the dough when necessary.

5 Place the oatcakes on the baking tray, prick twice with a fork then bake for 15–20 minutes until light golden. Cool on a wire rack for a few minutes.

(V) **Try this** For sweet versions, spread 1 teaspoon (20 g/¾ oz) of low fat soft cheese over each oatcake with a sliced strawberry, or use 1 teaspoon of chocolate hazelnut spread with three slices of banana.

For a savoury version, top with 1 teaspoon (20 g/¾ oz) of low fat soft cheese and a thin slice of cucumber.

Did you know?

Oatmeal is available as fine, medium and coarse; look out for the medium version for this recipe. These oatcakes will keep in an airtight container for up to 5 days.

Bagna cauda

Calories per serving 67

Takes 10 mins

Serves 6

75 g (2¾ oz) fresh white breadcrumbs
100 ml (3½ fl oz) skimmed milk
3 canned anchovies, drained and rinsed
4 teaspoons lemon juice
1 small garlic clove, crushed
freshly ground black pepper
paprika, to garnish (optional)
To serve
2 carrots, cut into sticks
1 cucumber, cut into sticks
1 large red pepper, cut into sticks
3 celery sticks, cut into thinner sticks

Serve each portion of this popular creamy Italian anchovy dip with the vegetable sticks and two 15 g (½ oz) breadsticks.

1 Put the breadcrumbs in a food processor with the milk, anchovies, lemon juice and garlic. Season with black pepper, then whizz until smooth and creamy.

2 Spoon into a bowl and sprinkle paprika over the top, if using.

3 Divide the vegetable sticks between each person and serve with the bagna cauda.

Cook's tip The dip will keep for up to 3 days if stored in an airtight container in the fridge.

Celery with blue cheese dip

Calories per serving 72

Takes 5 mins

V   **Serves 1**

15 g (½ oz) spreadable blue cheese, such as
    creamy Saint Agur
1 teaspoon lemon juice
1 tablespoon 0% fat Greek yogurt
2 celery sticks, trimmed
freshly ground black pepper

You can't beat the old favourites such as these filled celery sticks. You could also serve the blue cheese dip with vegetable crudités, such as carrots, pepper, cucumber or baby corn.

1 In a bowl, mix together the cheese, lemon juice and yogurt. Season with black pepper.

2 Spoon the mixture along the length of the celery before eating.

Mediterranean toasts

Calories per serving 238
Takes 10 mins
(V)   Serves 1

1 medium slice wholemeal bread
½ small avocado, stone removed
1 teaspoon lemon juice
1 small garlic clove
1 tomato, sliced into rounds
balsamic vinegar, for drizzling
freshly ground black pepper
fresh basil leaves, to garnish

Toasting the bread in a hot griddle pan gives it a lovely, slightly charred flavour and appearance but you can also toast it in the usual way.

1 Heat a griddle pan until hot. Place the bread in the pan, press down to flatten it then griddle for 2–3 minutes on each side until toasted. Alternatively, toast the bread under the grill or in the toaster.

2 Meanwhile, using a spoon, scoop the avocado out of its skin and mash with the lemon juice.

3 Rub the garlic over one side of the toasted bread then discard. Top the bread with the avocado. Arrange the tomato on top and drizzle over a little balsamic vinegar.

4 Season with black pepper, halve diagonally then scatter over a few basil leaves before serving.

(V) **Try this** Instead of the avocado, you could spread 2 tablespoons of low fat vegetarian pâté over the toast.

Sardines and salsa on toasted bagel

Calories per serving 167
Takes 10 mins
                                       Serves 2

1 Weight Watchers bagel, halved
1 tomato, de-seeded and diced
1 cm (½ inch) cucumber, de-seeded and diced
1 teaspoon diced red onion
1 tablespoon chopped fresh parsley
1 teaspoon lemon juice
a splash of Tabasco
95 g can boneless sardines in tomato sauce
freshly ground black pepper

Canned fish makes a handy storecupboard standby.

1 Lightly toast the bagel halves under the grill or in a toaster.

2 Meanwhile, mix together the diced tomato, cucumber, red onion, parsley, lemon juice and Tabasco. Season with black pepper to taste.

3 Divide the sardines between each bagel half. Top with the tomato salsa before serving.

(V) **Try this** For a vegetarian alternative, omit the sardines. Spread each half of toasted bagel with 1 teaspoon of reduced fat houmous then top with the tomato salsa.

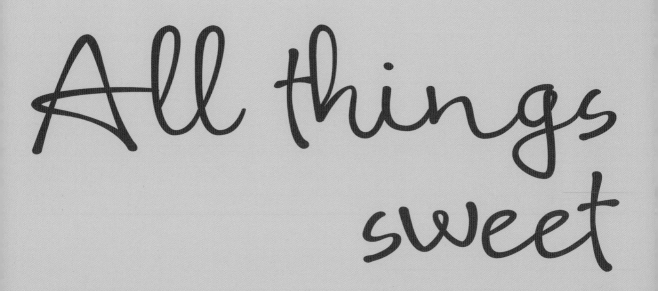

All things sweet

Spiced chocolate pots with filo sticks on page 144

These delectable desserts are fabulous anytime – they're great for a summer barbecue but they're just as scrummy after a warming Sunday lunch too. Sit back and enjoy the zingy Pimm's and Lemonade Jellies or the cooling Vanilla and Coconut Balls with Mango. It's hard to beat the Apple Syrup Puddings but if you really want to impress friends and family, the Blueberry Cheesecake Brûlées will do the trick.

Summer slush

Calories per serving 85

20 mins prep + 4 hrs freezing +

20 mins softening

V ❄

Serves 4

900 g (2 lb) honeydew melon
½ cucumber, peeled, de-seeded and chopped
juice of 2 limes
3 tablespoons icing sugar
finely shredded zest of 1 lime, to decorate

A refreshing granita is perfect for a hot summer's day or after a spicy curry.

1 Halve the melon, remove the seeds then, using a spoon, scoop out the flesh. Put the melon in a blender with the cucumber and blend to a coarse purée. Stir in the lime juice and sugar.

2 Tip the mixture into a freezerproof container with a lid and freeze for 2 hours then, using a fork, stir to break up the ice crystals. Return to the freezer for another 2 hours or until frozen.

3 To serve, leave to soften for 20 minutes then scrape the top of the ice with a fork to form loose crystals. Spoon the granita into glasses then top with a few shreds of lime zest before serving.

Barbecued fruit with vanilla cream

Calories per serving 152

Takes 30 mins

V

Serves 4

1 tablespoon soft brown sugar
2 teaspoons vanilla extract
4 nectarines, halved and stoned
4 plums, halved and stoned
200 g (7 oz) cherries
For the vanilla cream
100 g (3½ oz) 0% fat Greek yogurt
1 tablespoon half fat crème fraîche
1 teaspoon icing sugar

It's best to cook the fruit in a foil tray to separate it from the direct heat of the barbecue and other foods that may have been cooked on it.

1 Light the barbecue or heat a grill to medium-high.

2 Mix together the soft brown sugar and half of the vanilla extract. Put the fruit in a bowl, spoon over the brown sugar mixture and turn until coated. Set aside for 15 minutes.

3 Arrange the nectarines and plums cut side down in a foil tray (see Cook's tip). Barbecue or grill over a medium-high heat, for about 6 minutes, depending on the heat of the barbecue and the ripeness of the fruit, until caramelised. Alternatively, cook for the same length of time under the grill. Turn over then add the cherries and cook for another 4 minutes until juicy and softened.

4 Meanwhile, to make the cream, mix together all the ingredients with the remaining vanilla extract in a bowl. Serve the fruit with the vanilla cream.

Cook's tip If you don't have a foil tray, you can make one using a thick sheet of foil and turn up the sides to form a 1 cm (½ inch) lip all the way around.

Pimm's and lemonade jellies

Calories per serving 44

Takes 15 mins + 4½ hrs chilling

Serves 4

6 sheets gelatine
75 ml (3 fl oz) Pimm's
375 ml (13 fl oz) low calorie lemonade
75 g (2¾ oz) strawberries
4 thin ribbons cucumber
4 small fresh mint leaves, to decorate

These pretty jellies will liven up any summer barbecue. Prepare them in advance, if you wish, and decorate just before serving.

1 Put the gelatine in a bowl, cover with cold water and leave to soak for 5 minutes.

2 Remove the gelatine from the bowl and, using your hands, squeeze out any excess water. Put the gelatine in a saucepan with half of the Pimm's and simmer over a gentle heat, stirring, until the gelatine dissolves.

3 Remove from the heat then pour in the rest of the Pimm's with the lemonade and stir until combined. Pour 60 ml (2½ fl oz) of the Pimm's mixture into each of the four small glasses. Chill for 30 minutes to set slightly.

4 Halve two of the strawberries and reserve them to decorate. Slice the remaining strawberries, and divide between the four glasses and pour the remaining jelly mixture over the fruit. Return to the fridge and chill until set, about 4 hours.

5 Serve decorated with the reserved strawberries, cucumber and fresh mint leaves.

Pineapple with pistachios and ginger cream

Calories per serving 129

Takes 15 mins

(V)

Serves 6

1 pineapple, unpeeled, cored removed and cut into
    6 wedges
calorie controlled cooking spray
1 teaspoon ground ginger
30 g (1¼ oz) pistachios, chopped roughly

For the ginger cream
200 g (7 oz) 0% fat Greek yogurt
2 balls of stem ginger in syrup, drained and
    chopped finely
2 tablespoons syrup from the stem ginger

Pineapple and ginger complement each other perfectly and make an impressively simple dessert for a summer barbecue.

1 To make the ginger cream, mix together the yogurt, stem ginger and syrup in a bowl.

2 Spray the pineapple with the cooking spray. While the barbecue is still hot, place the pineapple directly on to the rack and cook for 2 minutes on each side until caramelised and slightly charred in places. Alternatively, cook the pineapple under a preheated grill for 3 minutes on each side.

3 Serve a wedge of pineapple per person with a good spoonful of the ginger cream. Sprinkle some ground ginger over the top and scatter the pistachios over the cream.

Raspberry verrine

Calories per serving 186

Takes 15 mins

V   **Serves 2**

30 g (1¼ oz) whole rolled porridge oats
3 teaspoons maple syrup
5 pecan halves (about 15 g/½ oz)
140 g (5 oz) fat free fromage frais
125 g (4½ oz) raspberries

1 Put the oats in a dry frying pan and toast over a medium-low heat for 5 minutes, stirring regularly until light golden. Tip the oats into a bowl and pour in 1 teaspoon of the maple syrup. Stir until coated and leave to cool.

2 Meanwhile, put the pecans in a bowl with 1 teaspoon of maple syrup and turn until coated. Put the pecans in the pan and toast for 2 minutes, turning once, until golden. Remove the nuts from the pan, but set aside two pecans and then roughly chop the remaining ones.

3 Mix the cooled oats and chopped pecans together. Add a spoonful to each glass and top with some of the fromage frais and half of the raspberries. Top with the remaining oats and pecans, fromage frais and raspberries, reserving a few to decorate.

4 Drizzle over the rest of the maple syrup then decorate with the raspberries and reserved pecans. Serve immediately.

Spiced chocolate pots with filo sticks

Calories per serving 212

Takes 30 mins + 30 mins chilling

V   **Serves 4**

75 g (2¾ oz) plain chocolate
2 eggs, separated
2 tablespoons caster sugar
½ teaspoon allspice
½ teaspoon ground cinnamon
1 teaspoon vanilla extract
4 tablespoons Weight Watchers reduced fat
   thick cream

For the filo sticks

1 x 15 g (½ oz) filo sheet, measuring 24 cm x 26 cm
   (9½ x 10½ inches), halved crossways
calorie controlled cooking spray
½ teaspoon clear honey

1 Preheat the oven to Gas Mark 6/200°C/fan oven 180°C. To make the filo sticks, lie one half of the filo on a work surface, spray with the cooking spray then fold the filo in half lengthways, repeating twice to make a 1 cm (½ inch) wide long strip. Repeat with the remaining half of filo pastry.

2 Cut each filo stick in half to make four sticks in total. Brush the tops of the filo with the honey and place on a non stick baking sheet. Bake in the oven for 10–12 minutes.

3 Put the chocolate in a heatproof bowl and place it over a saucepan of gently simmering water. Stir once or twice until melted and then remove from the heat. Leave to cool slightly for 5 minutes.

4 Meanwhile, in a clean, grease-free bowl, whisk the egg whites until they form soft peaks. Continue to whisk while gradually adding the sugar to form stiff, glossy peaks.

5 Beat the egg yolks into the melted chocolate then stir in the spices, vanilla and cream. Using a metal spoon, gradually fold in the egg whites until mixed in. Spoon the mousse into the four 150 ml (5 fl oz) pots or ramekins. Chill until set then serve with one filo stick per person.

Cook's tip When melting the chocolate, don't let the bottom of the bowl touch the simmering water – you only need about 2.5 cm (1 inch) of water in the pan – or allow the steam to come into contact with the chocolate as it can 'seize' and become stiff and crumbly.

Apricot and chocolate bar

Calories per serving 159

Takes 20 mins + 1 hr chilling

(V)   **Serves 8**

150 g (5½ oz) plain chocolate (at least 70% cocoa
     solids)
60 g (2 oz) ready to eat dried apricots, chopped
     roughly
2 low fat digestive biscuits, broken into small
     pieces
2 egg whites
15 g (½ oz) white chocolate

Swirls of white chocolate with melted plain chocolate, crushed biscuits and chopped apricots are chilled into a tasty bar.

1 Line a 20 cm (8 inch) square baking dish with baking parchment.

2 Put the plain chocolate in a heatproof bowl, and place over a pan of gently simmering water – do not let the bottom of the bowl touch the water or the steam come into contact with the chocolate. Stir the chocolate once or twice until melted then remove from the heat and leave to cool slightly.

3 Stir the apricots and digestive biscuits into the chocolate.

4 In a clean, grease-free bowl, whisk the egg whites until they form stiff peaks. Gradually fold the egg whites into the chocolate mixture until combined then tip the mixture into the prepared dish, spreading it out into an even layer, about 1 cm (½ inch) thick and about 20 cm (8 inches) x 13 cm (5 inches). It won't fill the entire dish but that's ok.

5 Melt the white chocolate in the same way as the plain chocolate, stirring occasionally. Drizzle the melted white chocolate on top. Chill in the fridge for about 1 hour or until set.

6 Once set, cut the chocolate bar into eight pieces and store in a lidded container in the fridge until ready to eat.

(V) **Try this** You might like to replace the apricots with the same quantity of goji berries.

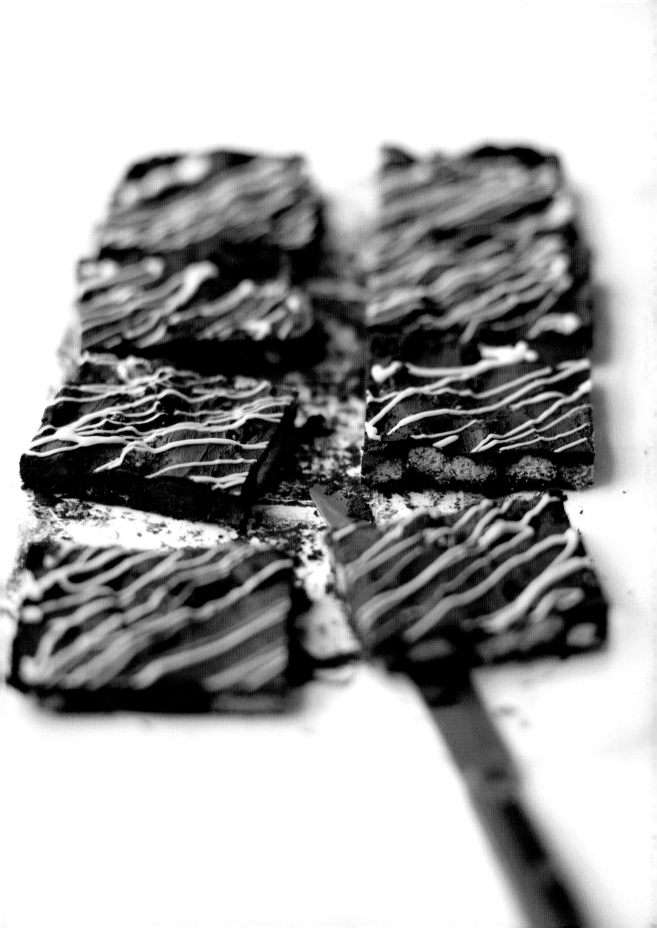

Vanilla and coconut balls with mango

Calories per serving 98

Takes 20 mins

V ❋   **Serves 4**

4 tablespoons unsweetened desiccated coconut
4 x 40 g (1½ oz) balls of low fat vanilla ice cream,
    softened slightly
1 fresh mango, peeled, stoned and sliced thickly

This dessert is ideal after an oriental or spicy meal.

1 Put the coconut in a dry non stick frying pan and toast for 2 minutes, stirring occasionally, until light golden. Transfer to a plate and leave to cool for 5 minutes.

2 Take a scoop of ice cream and roll it in the toasted coconut until coated then repeat with the rest of the ice cream. If time allows, return the ice cream to the freezer for 10 minutes to harden slightly.

3 Divide the mango between four plates. Place the coconut coated ice cream by the side of the mango and serve immediately.

Hot banana splits

Calories per serving 222

15 mins prep, 20 mins cooking

V   **Serves 2**

2 just ripe bananas, unpeeled
25 g (1 oz) walnut halves
2 teaspoons honey

To help the bananas hold their shape after baking, it's best to use fruit that is only just ripe instead of overly so. They're yummy with a 60 g (2 oz) scoop of low fat vanilla ice cream per person.

1 Preheat the oven to Gas Mark 5/190°C/fan oven 170°C. Place the unpeeled bananas on a baking tray and bake for 18–20 minutes until the skin has blackened and the fruit is tender inside.

2 While the bananas are baking, toast the walnuts in a dry non stick frying pan for 4–5 minutes until slightly golden. Leave to cool then chop roughly.

3 To serve, place a banana on each plate and make a slit along the curve of the fruit and open it out slightly. Scatter the walnuts over the top then drizzle with the honey.

Blueberry cheesecake brûlées

Calories per serving 219

Takes 25 mins + 1 hr chilling

V   **Serves 4**

1 teaspoon cornflour
150 g (5½ oz) blueberries
2 tablespoons caster sugar
125 g (4½ oz) low fat soft cheese
150 g (5½ oz) 0% fat Greek yogurt
1 teaspoon vanilla extract
grated zest of 1 lemon
½ teaspoon ground cinnamon
4 light digestive biscuits, crumbled
4 teaspoons demerara sugar

The beauty of this dessert is that it can be made up to a day in advance and it still tastes great.

1 Mix the cornflour to a paste with 1 teaspoon of water. Put the blueberries in a pan with 1 tablespoon of the caster sugar and 1 tablespoon of water. Cook over a medium-low heat, covered, for 4 minutes until the berries are soft and juicy. Stir in the cornflour paste and cook, stirring, for 1–2 minutes until thickened. Leave to cool.

2 Meanwhile, mix together the soft cheese, yogurt, vanilla, lemon zest and cinnamon with the remaining caster sugar.

3 Divide the crumbled digestives between four large ramekins and top with the blueberries then the cheese mixture. Smooth the top then chill for 30 minutes.

4 Preheat the grill to high. Place the ramekins on a baking tray, sprinkle the tops with the demerara sugar. Put some water in a spray bottle and then mist the tops of the ramekins with a spray of water to help the sugar to caramelise.

5 Place the ramekins under the grill for 2–3 minutes or until the sugar has melted, taking care with them as they can burn. Return the ramekins to the fridge and chill for another 30 minutes before serving.

Cook's tip The brûlées can be served after grilling too if you wish, but leave the sugar to cool slightly and then serve them warm.

Top tips...

If you can't find fresh blueberries, frozen are just as good and they don't need to be defrosted before use. The blueberry sauce can also be stored in an airtight jar in the fridge for up to 1 week.

Pear and berry pudding

Calories per serving 213

Takes 25 mins + overnight chilling

V ❄

Serves 9

3 pears, peeled, cored and chopped into small
    bite size pieces
500 g (1 lb 2 oz) frozen fruits of the forest
250 ml (9 fl oz) fresh orange juice
90 g (3¼ oz) caster sugar
1 teaspoon ground cinnamon
½ teaspoon allspice
450 g (1 lb) day-old sliced white bread, crusts
    removed

Serve with 30 g (1¼ oz) Weight Watchers Reduced Fat Thick Cream per person.

1 Put the pears, frozen fruit, orange juice, sugar and spices in a lidded saucepan and bring to the boil, then reduce the heat, part cover, and simmer for about 8 minutes or until tender and juicy. Strain the juice into a large jug.

2 Arrange half of the sliced bread in a 25 x 20 cm (10 x 8 inch) dish. Top with the cooked fruit and pour over enough of the strained juice to lightly soak the bread.

3 Place a second layer of bread on top of the fruit and pour some more of the juice over the top until the bread is ruby red (don't allow it to become too soggy) and you should have some juice left over. Press a sheet of baking parchment over the top of the bread and then weigh it down with some food cans or the weights from scales. Chill overnight.

4 To serve, divide into nine portions (three rows of three). Pour some of the reserved fruit juice over each serving.

Fruit and marshmallow skewers

Calories per serving 244

Takes 35 mins

V

Serves 4

2 just ripe nectarines, halved, stoned and each half
    cut into 4 pieces
200 g (7 oz) canned pineapple chunks in natural
    juice (about 12 pieces), drained
calorie controlled cooking spray
16 large marshmallows
For the chocolate sauce
50 g (1¾ oz) plain chocolate
200 ml (7 fl oz) semi skimmed milk
2 teaspoons cornflour
30 g (1¼ oz) caster sugar

Toasted marshmallows – what better way to finish a barbecue?

1 To make the sauce, melt the chocolate and half of the milk in a small saucepan over a low heat, stirring occasionally. Mix together the remaining milk, cornflour and sugar then stir into the pan. Warm through, stirring, until thickened to a sauce consistency. Pour into four ramekins. Set aside.

2 If using a grill, heat to a medium-high heat. Put the fruit in a bowl and spray with the cooking spray. Thread four chunks of nectarine and three of pineapple alternately on to four skewers.

3 Next, thread four marshmallows each on to the skewers.

4 Place the fruit skewers on the barbecue or under the grill and cook for about 8 minutes, turning occasionally, until they start to caramelise. Place each one on a serving plate while you cook the marshmallow skewers for about 3–4 minutes, turning occasionally, until they begin to turn gooey.

5 Serve one skewer per person accompanied by a pot of chocolate sauce for dunking.

Poached fruit with buttermilk snow

Calories per serving 152

Takes 30 mins + 5 hrs freezing +

20 mins softening

(V) (❄) buttermilk snow only   **Serves 2**

1 apple, peeled, cored and diced
1 pear, peeled, cored and diced
75 g (2¾ oz) rhubarb, trimmed and sliced into 1 cm
    (½ inch) pieces
50 ml (2 fl oz) fresh orange juice
1 star anise
2 teaspoons caster sugar
For the buttermilk snow
150 ml (5 fl oz) buttermilk
1 tablespoon icing sugar
½ teaspoon vanilla extract

Apple, pear and rhubarb make a delicious fruit compote and can be served warm or cold, while the buttermilk ice makes a refreshing alternative to cream or ice cream.

1 To make the buttermilk snow, mix together all the ingredients in a small freezerproof container and freeze for 2 hours until semi frozen. Stir with a fork to break up the ice crystals then return to the freezer for a further 2–3 hours until frozen.

2 To poach the fruit, put the apple, pear and rhubarb in a lidded saucepan with the orange juice, star anise and caster sugar. Bring up to the boil then reduce the heat to low, cover, and simmer for 10 minutes or until tender. Add a little water if the pan becomes too dry.

3 Remove the buttermilk snow from the freezer and leave to soften for 20 minutes. Remove the star anise from the pan, spoon the fruit and juice into two large ramekins or small bowls and leave to cool slightly for 10 minutes or until completely cold.

4 Scrape the top of the buttermilk with a fork to make ice crystals then spoon on top of the fruit. Serve immediately.

(V) **Try this** If rhubarb is out of season, you could swap it with the same weight of stoned cherries or double the quantity of apples or pears.

Did you know?

If you can't find buttermilk (which is usually available in the cream section in supermarkets), it's easy to make your own by mixing 150 ml (5 fl oz) plain yogurt with 1 teaspoon of lemon juice.

Apple syrup puddings

Calories per serving 324

20 mins prep, 35 mins cooking

(V)   **Serves 4**

75 g (2¾ oz) low fat spread, plus ½ teaspoon
for greasing
100 g (3½ oz) self raising flour
½ teaspoon baking powder
1 teaspoon ground cinnamon
75 g (2¾ oz) caster sugar
2 eggs, beaten lightly
1 teaspoon vanilla extract
3 tablespoons skimmed milk
1 apple, peeled and grated
4 teaspoons golden syrup

Serve these golden syrup topped puddings with 100 g (3½ oz) canned low fat custard each.

1 Preheat the oven to Gas Mark 4/180°C/fan oven 160°C. Lightly grease four 150 ml (5 fl oz) pudding moulds with a little low fat spread.

2 In a bowl, sift together the flour, baking powder and cinnamon.

3 In another mixing bowl, beat together the low fat spread and sugar until light and creamy – this takes about 5 minutes. Gradually beat in the eggs and if the mixture curdles, add a spoonful of the flour mixture.

4 Fold in the remaining flour mixture then stir in the vanilla and milk. Add the apple and stir until combined.

5 Spoon a teaspoon of the syrup into each pudding mould then top with the apple mixture. Place the moulds on a baking sheet and bake for 30–35 minutes until risen and golden. Leave to cool for a few minutes then run a knife around the edge of the pudding and tip out on to a plate. Serve immediately.

Make it quick...

A food processor or an electric hand whisk make easy work of preparing these delicious sponge puddings. Simply whisk the dry ingredients with the spread, sugar, eggs, vanilla and milk until smooth and creamy then stir in the apple.

Index